T0308778

WISCONSIN
COCKTAILS

WISCONSIN COCKTAILS

JEANETTE HURT

The University of Wisconsin Press

The University of Wisconsin Press
728 State Street, Suite 443
Madison, Wisconsin 53706
uwpress.wisc.edu

Gray's Inn House, 127 Clerkenwell Road
London EC1R 5DB, United Kingdom
eurospanbookstore.com

Illustrations by Gabriela Muñiz (except p242 by Tim Martin)

Printed in the United States of America
This book may be available in a digital edition.

Library of Congress Cataloging-in-Publication Data
Names: Hurt, Jeanette, author.
Title: Wisconsin cocktails / Jeanette Hurt.
Description: Madison, Wisconsin : The University of Wisconsin Press, [2020] |
    Includes index.
Identifiers: LCCN 2020004314 | ISBN 9780299328801 (cloth)
Subjects: LCSH: Cocktails—Wisconsin. | Drinking of alcoholic beverages—
    Wisconsin.
Classification: LCC TX951 .H874 2020 | DDC 641.87/409775—dc23

LC record available at https://lccn.loc.gov/2020004314

This book is dedicated to my cousins Barb and George and their lovely families: Victor and Victoria, Laura, Erika, and Stephanie. We will rock you!

CONTENTS

NO2

BLOODY MARYS, BEER CHASERS, AND RED ROBINS

NO3

THE TOM AND JERRY

NO4

BANSHEES, PINK SQUIRRELS, AND OTHER WILD CREATURES

NO5

HOT TODDIES, BUTTERED RUM, AND COFFEE COCKTAILS

N0 6
BRANDY SLUSHES, CHERRY BOUNCE, AND OTHER WISCONSIN DRINKING HABITS

N<u>O</u>7
NEW WISCONSIN COCKTAILS
OTHER DRINKS THAT AIM TO PUT
THE DAIRY STATE ON THE COCKTAIL MAP

NO 8

SPIRITFREE
NONALCOHOLIC COCKTAILS MADE WITH WISCONSIN INGREDIENTS

APPENDIX
WISCONSIN COCKTAIL AND CHEESE PAIRINGS

FOREWORD

Robert Simonson

When it comes to American drinking traditions, Wisconsin is a force unto itself. Other states and cities may have their cherished and time-honored sups: Kentucky its bourbon and Mint Julep; New Orleans its Sazerac and Ramos Gin Fizz; Washington, DC, its Gin Rickey. But no one matches the Badger State (well, maybe New Orleans) for the sheer number and longevity of its tippling habits.

That Wisconsinites have long exhibited a prodigious thirst has helped push this barroom supremacy along. Other factors include the state's strong German heritage and the great knowledge of brewing and distilling that came with it; the long winters, which require a fortifying nip or two to get through; and the no-nonsense, trend-adverse nature of the citizenry, who over the years have seen few reasons to change what ain't broken, drinking preferences included.

Wisconsin has long deserved a book devoted to its wide array of native quaffs, toasts, mixtures, and punches, and with *Wisconsin Cocktails* Jeanette Hurt has at last delivered one. Within these thirst-inducing pages you will discover the stories behind the brandy Old Fashioned, inarguably the unofficial state cocktail (FYI, for those who have never left that state, most people make their Old Fashioneds with whiskey); the once equally popular brandy Manhattan; the undyingly cherished holiday-season punch, the Tom and Jerry, a sort of hot egg nog; ice cream drinks, a dessert-like alcoholic specialty at bars and supper clubs in every Dairyland county (Grasshoppers here are made with ice cream, not the usual cream); the Pink Squirrel, a sweet rosy concoction that, if not invented in Wisconsin, has certainly been given a bigger bear's hug here than in any other state; Nelsen's Hall, an isolated bar on Washington Island, just off the tip of Door County, which happens to sell more Angostura bitters than any other tavern in the United States; and Wisconsin's uniquely overloaded Bloody Marys, which groan under more garnishes than any in the world and typically are served with a "snit" of beer on the side.

Behind all these drinks and more, Wisconsinites have valiantly stood through thick and thin, enjoying them year after year, payday after payday, tailgate after tailgate long after the rest of the world has moved on to the latest fly-by-night drinking fad. It can be argued that for decades Wisconsin singlehandedly kept the torch alight for classic drinks like the Old Fashioned and the Tom and Jerry, waiting patiently until the questing young bartenders of the current worldwide cocktail revival found the time to rediscover and repopularize them in the early years of this century. And thus what looked like stubborn, staid, midwestern cocktail-hour contrariness just a couple of decades ago now looks like the work of a prescient population who knew the swell from the swill. Loyalty and steadfastness has its rewards.

Robert Simonson, a native of Wisconsin, writes about cocktails for the *New York Times* and is the author of the books *The Old-Fashioned*, *A Proper Drink*, *Three-Ingredient Cocktails*, and *The Martini Cocktail*.

PREFACE

Four years ago, I started working on a book proposal called "The United Drinks of America," and the idea behind this proposed book was that every state has its own unique cocktail, and every state has its own unique drinking culture.

What I learned, from researching this idea, is that some drinks definitely were invented in some states—the Alabama Slammer, for example, was definitely invented in Alabama. The Sazerac (and the Hurricane and a whole bunch of other cocktails) were invented in New Orleans.

But while most states have some semblance of a drinking culture, it's not usually very interesting, or it's not really that different from many other states, and, despite some random memes and online articles, most states don't really have an official or even unofficial cocktail that practically everyone in the state either drinks or at least holds an opinion about.

This actually surprised me. Because I live in Wisconsin. Everyone here knows that the Old Fashioned is our unofficial state cocktail, and most of us hold strong opinions about how we should drink them— brandy or bourbon; sweet, sour, or pressed; and whether a cherry or pickled Brussels sprout or whatever should be served with it.

Not only that, Wisconsin never actually stopped making cocktails. While some states may have experienced what lofty craft mixologists consider to be the "Dark Age of Cocktails," aka, the 1970s and 1980s, we never did. Go to any dive bar, corner tavern, or sports bar anywhere in our state, practically, and the bartenders there should know how to make you a proper Old Fashioned (even if it's not muddled, and they add a cherry syrup or old-fashioned mix to make it quickly). They also should add more than a measly pickle to garnish your Bloody Mary, and they sure as heck know that every good Bloody deserves a beer chaser or snit, and even if they don't advertise it on their menu, they might just make you a proper Grasshopper, made with ice cream (and chances are, if they don't serve ice cream drinks, the place next door probably does).

We have cocktails that are so unique to Wisconsin that if we ask for them a certain way, whether we're in Las Vegas or Orlando, Manhattan or Miami, the bartender will go, "Oh, are you from Wisconsin?" And we really shouldn't be that surprised.

Simple Words about Simple Syrup: Or, Some Bartending Basics

Talk to any bartender or home bar enthusiast and they immediately understand what simple syrup is and why it's so necessary for almost any cocktail out there. But for the rest of us, simple syrup sounds like an elusive elixir—like bitters or tinctures or infused spirits—especially if the simple syrup is a flavored simple syrup like lavender simple syrup or ginger simple syrup or honey simple syrup. It's sometimes as intimidating as heck.

But really, simple syrup is just sugar water. That's right. It's sugar water. To make it, you just measure out equal parts sugar and water that's hot enough to dissolve it—so, to make about ½ cup of simple syrup, you just whisk together ½ cup of water and ½ cup of sugar.

You don't even have to warm it up in the microwave or boil it on the stove—you just have to have tap water that's hot enough for the sugar crystals to dissolve.

If you want it sweeter, you can increase the amount of sugar. Or you can use honey or maple syrup or brown sugar or basically any other kind of sweetener in place of the sugar. And if you want to get fancier, add some herbs or spices—about one tablespoon of herbs per cup of simple syrup—and let it steep for about twenty to thirty minutes, then strain.

You can actually buy simple syrup from some fancy liquor stores, but you don't need to—just mix up equal parts sugar and water. When I make a big batch of simple syrup, I pour the extra syrup into plastic bags, label them with the date, then freeze them. They basically turn into a slushy sugar mixture, and I can then thaw out an ounce or two as needed. I've kept my simple syrup and flavored simple syrups in the freezer for up to six months.

Some recipes call for certain flavored syrups, so those recipes follow the cocktail recipes. But most recipes just call for a basic simple syrup. Now, if you follow the simple syrup recipe exactly and the cocktail recipe exactly and it doesn't taste sweet enough, you have two choices: increase the amount of sugar in your simple syrup (I'd start with ¾ cup water to 1 cup sugar) or just increase the amount of simple syrup in the cocktail itself in quarter-ounce increments. It really is that simple.

A Word about Brand Name Liquors:
Or, More Bartending Basics

In this book there are some recipes that call out specific brand names of different spirits and liqueurs or bitters or cherries. The reason for this is that the bartender or distiller used these specific brands when they created that recipe. But just because they used them, you certainly don't have to use them.

In fact, you should use whatever is stocked in your home bar, whatever your favorite brand is, or whatever happened to be on sale at the grocery store this week. While there can be taste differences among brands—and sometimes there's a pretty remarkable difference—you don't have to use any specific brand to make any cocktail in this book.

And while there are some very specific spirits or liqueurs that are made only by certain distilleries—Kringle Cream is only made by Nordic Distillery, Chai liqueur is only made by Twisted Path, and Great Lakes' Good Land is the only cranberry liqueur I've seen on the market—you can easily sub out one liquor or spirit for another, and you can swap out one type of cherries for another or one type of bitters for another. And if you hate gin, you can swap it out for another clear spirit like vodka or rum. And if you really hate whiskey but love brandy, go ahead and make a brandy sour instead of a whiskey sour. Or a vodka sour. The cocktail might not have the same flavor profile as the original, but so long as you like it, it doesn't matter.

The point is—you can and should go by your own particular preferences. This is true at your home bar, your friend's backyard barbecue, and also at whatever bar or restaurant you happen to be frequenting at the moment. If you don't like a drink made a certain way, please tell your bartender—or send it back if you think it should be sweeter or have more of a sour tang to it or if it simply isn't to your liking. While there are definitely some snobby bartenders out there—and they often prefer to call themselves by the loftier term *mixologist*—most bartenders are caring, kind people, and many of them have told me that they are happy when their customers are happy. That means, they never take offense at any request, whether it's for a sweeter drink or a pickled Brussels sprout to accompany a Manhattan. And most of them would not take offense if you decided to make their cocktail recipe using a different brand.

This book celebrates our rich history of cocktails, and it also delves into the history of why and how we came to drink our drinks the way we drink them. So, cheers, and On Wisconsin!

WISCONSIN
COCKTAILS

№ 1

THE WISCONSIN, ER, BRANDY, OLD FASHIONED

THOUGH SOME NATIONAL PUBLICATIONS AND ONLINE ARTICLES HAVE SAID WISCONSIN'S UNOFFICIAL COCKTAIL IS THE BLOODY MARY OR THE WHISKEY SOUR, TRUE WISCONSINITES KNOW IT'S THE OLD FASHIONED. AND IT'S NOT THE OLD FASHIONED THAT YOU ORDER EVERYWHERE ELSE IN THE COUNTRY. IF YOU ORDER AN OLD FASHIONED ANY-WHERE ELSE, THEY'LL GIVE YOU A STRAIGHTFORWARD COCKTAIL MADE WITH JUST BITTERS, WHISKEY (MOST LIKELY RYE OR BOURBON), AND JUST A TOUCH OF SUGAR, GARNISHED WITH AN ORANGE OR LEMON PEEL.

Don't get me wrong—this Old Fashioned (as folks in other states call it) is a delicious, if very boozy, drink. But that's not how we mostly make our Old Fashioneds or any derivatives thereof in Wisconsin.

Guy Rehorst, who opened up the very first distillery in Wisconsin since Prohibition when he opened the Great Lakes Distillery in Milwaukee in 2004, remembers ordering the simple version of a Wisconsin Old Fashioned—a brandy and seven, or equal parts brandy and 7-Up—in Toronto when he was just out of college. "The waiter brought me a snifter of brandy and a glass of 7-Up, and he was abso-lutely horrified when I poured them together," Rehorst says.

But he never got any weird looks when he ordered them back home because basically, a brandy and seven is an Old Fashioned with-out the sugar, the cherries, or the orange.

A true and properly made Wisconsin Old Fashioned is made by

muddling cherries and oranges with bitters and sugar (or a simple syrup), brandy (or whiskey), then topped with sweet soda or sour soda or seltzer or a combination of sweet and seltzer (press), then garnished with cherries and oranges or olives or pickled onions or even pickled Brussels sprouts.

When you order an Old Fashioned in Wisconsin, the bartender asks a series of questions to determine how you want your drink made. "People order Old Fashioneds made with gin or vodka or rum," says Scotty McCormick, head bartender at Lola's Restaurant at the Osthoff Resort in Elkhart Lake. "I had an older gentleman just the other weekend order a vodka Old Fashioned with extra olives, and he said 'I've been drinking them [this way] for forty years.' And I said, 'Well, I've been making them for forty years, and this is the first time I've heard that.'"

Elizabeth Behrens, bartender at Bar West at the Abbey Resort in Fontana, says that when she moved back to Wisconsin—she grew up partly in northern Wisconsin—after bartending for three years in Texas, she had an Old Fashioned learning curve. "They have so many different ways of ordering an Old Fashioned here I was like, what?" Behrens says. "It's definitely a Wisconsin thing, and even if my guests aren't from Wisconsin, they know Wisconsin is known for their brandy Old Fashioneds so they want to try one."

But how did we get to this point, of having a bartender ask us a series of questions concerning how we want our Old Fashioned made? In the rest of the country, the Old Fashioned was, really, the very first cocktail invented. A simple concoction of spirits, sugar, and bitters arrived on the scene sometime between the late eighteenth and early nineteenth centuries, and while the stories of who and where and how it was invented remain quite muddled—Was it London? New York? New Orleans? (my favorite tale is that it was invented by tavern keeper and former sutler, someone who outfitted our troops with booze, Catherine Hustler in New York during the American Revolution)—somehow, it showed up, and when it came into being, people just called it a cocktail. Then, later during the nineteenth century, bartenders at saloons got creative, and they started mixing other things into their cocktails, and then customers, who yearned for that simpler combination, started asking for cocktails made the old fashioned way, and that is how the Old Fashioned cocktail came to be named.

While this genesis story works for the rest of the country, it doesn't explain how we started drinking our Old Fashioneds, nor does it explain our Old Fashioned's origins.

Korbel and the Columbian Exposition: Or, The Oft-Told Story about Our Brandy Addiction

There's one oft-told story—and it's been repeated in practically every story written in the last ten years about Wisconsin and the brandy Old Fashioned, whether written by a Wisconsin writer or someone from out of state—and that story goes something like this:

Three Czech brothers—Francis, Anton, and Joseph Korbel—had expanded from their initial California lumber and sawmill operations into farming, including grape growing, and they eventually became one of Sonoma County's first winemakers in 1882. Seven years after they began making wine, they moved into brandy, but their brandy wasn't selling as well as their sparkling wines. So, the good brothers

Old Fashioned at the Del-Bar (Del-Bar)

Korbel thought it might be wise to take their brandy on the road . . . to the World's Columbian Exposition in Chicago.

During the six months this world's fair was held in 1893, some twenty-seven million people—a quarter of the country's population

Old Fashioned at Nelsen's Hall
(Kyle Edwards)

at the time—enjoyed some sixty-five thousand items exhibited in the White City. Fairgoers got to ride the first Ferris Wheel, walk on "moveable sidewalks," and see how the first zipper—er, "clasp locker"—worked. They tasted Cracker Jack, Juicy Fruit, and Cream of Wheat. They also clamored for Aunt Jemima's pancake flour (so much that former slave and Chicagoan Nancy Green had to have special guards protect her and her exhibit as she demoed the pancakes), and they loved the taste of Pabst so much they awarded this Milwaukee brewer a ribbon. Not only that, but they tasted the very first brownies at the Women's Pavilion, created at the behest of Bertha Palmer of the Palmer House Hotel.

With Wisconsin's close proximity to Illinois and at least four major railroads offering passenger service between Chicago and several Wisconsin destinations, it's assumed that a good number of our state's residents visited the fair. And it's also practically a given that if they were at the fair, then they had to have run into and tried the Korbel brothers' distilled grape elixir. Because many Wisconsinites boasted German heritage—and good Germans always have preferred brandy to whiskey—it's believed that this is the origin of our brandy obsession.

This story has been told over and over again in magazines, newspapers, blogs, websites, and even in some Wisconsin history books. And I have to be honest: I myself repeated it in a story I wrote in 2017 for *Tales of the Cocktail* online magazine. The fact is, it's a great story—it's got some history, it seems logical, and it sounds like it could very well be true.

So much so, that it's not just writers like me who have retold it. It's also a story that bartenders across the state love to tell—and retell as they dash Angostura bitters into sugar cubes and as they muddle this bittersweetness with maraschino cherries and orange slices.

But just as maraschino cherries—and their FD&C Red 40 dye—have little semblance to fresh cherries growing on Door County trees, so does this White City story relate to the history of brandy in Wisconsin.

How This Story Grows:
Or, Brandy's Tall Tale

While Pabst did win an award at the fair (gold, not blue as the name suggests, but the marketing savvy Captain Frederick Pabst later started tying blue ribbons around his award-winning brewski), this Korbel story inflates the importance of brandy at the fair. It's turned this story into more of a legend. Or tall tale. And like so many myths, it's based in fact but it's also mingled in conjecture and then spun into something that's larger than life.

This brandy belief actually starts with an article published in the *Northwest Herald* of Crystal Lake, Illinois, on February 3, 2009. This nonbylined missive points to President Barack Obama's congressional luncheon following his inauguration, and how Korbel was the champagne served. It goes on to reveal a Chicago connection—that Korbel's big break in brandy selling came at the Columbia Exposition. Without any transition, it then mentions, "The many Germans who saw the world's fair in Chicago became Korbel's best brandy customers. Even today, Wisconsin with its large German population, still buys the most Korbel brandy of any state. The battleship *Wisconsin* was christened in 1899 with a bottle of Korbel Viking Champagne." (Actually, the state-named battleship was launched in 1943 and commissioned in 1944 during World War II.)

This information is published in a newspaper so it must be true, right? Well, apparently, the unbylined writer or writers at the *Northwest Herald* didn't follow the old Chicago journalism adage—if your mother says she loves you, check it out—because when I tried to fact-check this story with Korbel executives, they had never heard of Korbel Viking Champagne, nor could they with any absolute certainty say that the world's fair was the reason why Wisconsinites buy so much brandy. "We can't confirm that," says Margie Healy, vice president of communications at Korbel.

Now, while Korbel executives won't outright say this didn't happen, they also don't deny it, because, as this story gets repeated, their brand is promoted, and Korbel is, in fact, a beloved brandy within Wisconsin. While this misinformation could have just stayed in the Flatlands south of us, a Madison writer may have spied an earlier version of this story.

Apparently, this story—or a very similarly worded story—inspired Jerry Minnich to pen an opinion piece entitled "The Brandy

Old-Fashioned: Solving the Mystery Behind Wisconsin's Real State Drink." Minnich describes his personal quest into the origins of the Old Fashioned in the July 30, 2004, issue of the *Isthmus*. "For more than thirty years, I have wondered how this came to be. Why brandy?" Minnich describes how he had just finished reading Eric Larson's *The Devil in the White City* when he discovered the fair-Wisconsin connection.

Though Larson never mentioned brandy in his tale about a spooky serial killer, his bestseller got Minnich surfing the web for other food-stuffs mentioned in the book, and that's how he found that story in the *Northwest Herald*, about Korbel and the Columbian Exposition. Minnich quotes parts of the story, word for word, then writes "Eureka! This explains everything! The German population, which was much higher in 1893 than it is today. And the brand dominance of Korbel."

Minnich's opinion piece directly mentions that he read an article published by the *Northwest Herald*, but he reports that it was published on June 8, 2004. Though it seems he read the same story I tracked down, the story I found (and the only story a local research librarian could track down) was dated February 3, 2009, published a full five years later than the article he referenced. At several points in his story, Minnich quotes the story he found in the *Northwest Herald*, and his direct quotes from the story match the same exact words of the story I discovered. Since the story in the *Northwest Herald* archives at the Crystal Lake Library was listed as having been penned by "columnists," likely it was first published earlier, then simply updated for Obama's inauguration.

Flaws in the Korbel Theory

While the entire Korbel–Columbian Exposition connection sounds quite plausible, it's not exactly what happened. The entrepreneurial Korbel brothers did exhibit their brandy at the fair, but according to the Final Report of the California World's Fair Commission, published in 1896, so did twenty-five—twenty-five!—other California winemakers, including German immigrant winemakers. It's worth noting that some other winemakers exhibited not one but up to four different kinds of brandy, and Korbel only brought along one. But one thing is important to note: of these twenty-five winemakers showcasing their brandy at the fair, Korbel is the only one that is still making brandy today.

California brandy likely did wow Germans at the fair, but these Columbian brandy exhibits probably had a bigger impact on the actual country of Germany than on immigrants in Wisconsin or anywhere else in the country. That's because in 1894, newspapers reported that 313,445 gallons of brandy were shipped from San Francisco to Germany, with 409 barrels earmarked for the German army to use in its hospitals. It was the largest shipment of American brandy, from any American port, and press at the time remarked how rapidly the German appetite for American brandy was growing. Records don't reveal which winemakers in California shipped their brandy to Germany, but the same story noted that while Germans adored American brandy, Americans still preferred the French stuff. And that story didn't mention Wisconsin at all.

Some California brandy did make it to Wisconsin after the fair. An advertisement in the *Milwaukee Journal* in 1894 touted the large stock of California wines and brandy at the August Grenlich company on Fourth Street. Besides its thirty-one brands of California wines, it also boasted "California brandy, the medicinal properties of which have been recognized by the German government's purchasing of nine thousand barrels for use in military hospitals is kept on hand; besides choice brands of Bourbon, kept on hand in large quantities." And it's worth noting that this advertisement didn't mention Korbel by name.

While it's totally possible that Korbel may have sold brandy to Wisconsinites after the fair—and the company doesn't have records that date that far back—there's another reason to challenge the Korbel theory. Korbel actually stopped making brandy during Prohibition. It wasn't until the 1960s, after the winery's new owner, Adolph Heck, took over, that brandy-making resumed. That means, even if Wisconsin folks drank Korbel, they didn't drink it for at least thirty years. And as most Wisconsinites might surmise, not too many folks stopped drinking—whatever beverages they were drinking—during Prohibition.

Wisconsin Boasts Thirsty Brandy Drinking Roots

The last conundrum of the Korbel theory is that it proposes brandy-drinking either started or increased because of the Columbian Exposition. Though Wisconsinites definitely did drink brandy during and after 1893, our grape-tinged roots extend much further back in time. From the various—and numerous—mentions in newspapers across the state, brandy consumption has been a part of our culture for a long, long time. In fact, an exhaustive records search of nineteenth-century newspapers reveals that our ancestors drank brandy even before Wisconsin became a state in 1848.

Sometimes, brandy showed up in police blotter items—like the time a servant girl stole twenty-eight bottles of brandy, along with five boxes of cigars, or when a man asked for a glass of brandy, downed it, and then reached over the bar to steal money from a saloon along Water Street in Milwaukee. Other times, it was mentioned in passing under items like "SUPPOSED TO BE TRUE,—A Boston paper says that a lady who can't *eat* mince pies without brandy, can drink brandy without mince pies."

Or, just as an aside, "The *Wisconsin* swallows, horns and all, the ridiculous story about Horace Greely's appearance at a ball in N.Y.—drinking brandy and water, dancing the Polka, etc."

It showed up in short fiction—about a certain Mrs. Caudle who didn't like drinking and referred to it in seething terms. "I should like to know how many of you would care for what you call rational conversation if you had it without your filthy brandy and water; yes, and your more filthy tobacco smoke."

It showed up in poetry in an 1850 edition of the *Milwaukee Sentinel and Gazette*:

> Men brandy drink, and never think
> That girls at all can tell it;
> They don't suppose a woman's nose
> Was ever made to smell it.

And it's even mentioned in humor in another 1850 issue of *Milwaukee Sentinel and Gazette*: "OUT OF AMMUNITION.—The St. Paul *Chronicle* says that a hunting party of six left that town, recently, for a sporting excursion to Rush river, but having *only* 15 gallons of brandy with them, had to return on the eighth day, for a further supply of 'necessaries.'"

Druggists advertised in the classified section that they had "New Holland Gin, Also Cognac, Brandy." And there were multiple advertisements for Catawba, Ohio, brandy.

While the many brandy mentions might make it seem that we were the largest market for distilled grape juice, not a single Wisconsin city was listed in a national article that ran in 1899 about "CITIES THAT DRINK HARD." That story declares that the "leading brandy town for its size in the country is Detroit." The story explained that those hearty Michigan folks drank brandy because of their proximity to Canada. It also reported that Chicagoans, apparently, drank more beer than any other city, but it made no mention of its proximity to Milwaukee.

No matter what folks outside the state thought, Wisconsinites did consume plenty of brandy—by the glass and sometimes by the bottle. We drank it for medicinal purposes. We drank it in flips and nogs and punches, and we used it in mincemeat and sauces.

We even drank it in cocktails. In fact, one of the earliest references to Wisconsin and brandy comes in the form of a humorous rant against the temperance movement, published in 1846 in the *Wisconsin Herald*: "Lemonade took the floor; but was hissed down. Hard Cider got up with thunder scowling on his brow, and smacked his lips and swore he *would* speak. Gin Sling and Brandy Cocktail at the same time calming the floor. The confusion became terrific. The chairman cried order! Order! And decided against old Hard Cider, against whom he has had a grudge ever since the Presidential campaign of 1840 and gave his half brother Brandy Cocktail the floor."

Unfortunately, this poetic reference didn't include a recipe for such cocktails. Likely, the writer was referring to a cocktail that might have been similar to the one Jerry Thomas included in the very first cocktail book published in the United States. Thomas, who was a bartender long before he became an author, published the first edition of *The Bar-Tender's Guide: How to Mix Drinks or The Bon Vivant's Companion* in 1862, and his recipe for the Brandy Cocktail is straightforward:

> (Use small bar-glass.)
> Take 3 or 4 dashes of gum syrup.
> 2 dashes of bitters (Boker's or Angostura).
> 1 wine-glass of brandy.
> 1 or 2 dashes of Curaçao.
>
> Fill the glass one-third full of shaved ice, shake up well and strain into a cocktail glass. Twist a small piece of lemon rind in it and serve.

His recipe for the whiskey cocktail, which later evolved into the Old Fashioned, is very similar, except it uses only Boker's Bitters and does not include any dashes of Curaçao.

The Original "Wisconsin" Old Fashioned

Curiously enough, by the end of the nineteenth century we didn't put brandy in a very popular drink at the time. What was that drink? It was called the Old Fashioned. An enterprising *Milwaukee Journal* reporter noted that there was a new cocktail revolution afoot—in 1894. "There does not seem to be any falling off in the consumption of the hops product, while there is an apparent increase along other lines.

Old Fashioned and Cosmo at the Del-Bar (Del-Bar)

With the increase of the American element and the acclimating of the young German American portion of the community, there follows a branching off into the undiscovered fields of speculation and exploration. Beer was good enough for their fathers, but for them there are other worlds to conquer. Therefore a sort of revolution has resulted in the saloon business of Milwaukee. . . . Beer was too tame for these and they wanted it 'straight,' or indulged in the mysterious cocktail."

This reporter explained how every barkeeper comes up with his own individual formulas for cocktails, and he then mentioned several popular drinks at the time, including a "bracer" called the Morning Glory, which contained "absinthe mainly, anisette, a modicum of brandy and fizzed with a syphon seltzer."

Old Passions Old Fashioned at Great Lakes Distillery (Great Lakes Distillery)

Other drinks like the Dream, the New Orleans Fizz, the Willy Waugh, and the Sub Rosa are also delineated. "Then there is the old-fashioned Cocktail. It is one hundred years old, but has recently come into favor again. The manufacture is simple. Place a little water in the bottom of a glass, a lump of loaf sugar, a few drops of Angostura bitters, crush a bit of lemon peel, ice and whisky at discretion. It is said to be very palatable and encouraging."

What this means is, more than one hundred years ago, Wisconsinites drank Old Fashioneds the way the rest of the country drank and still drinks them: strong, with whiskey and without fruit. So, the first two questions are: When and how did Wisconsinites change their spirited allegiances? And how did they change the formula of the drink?

The Gradual Growth of Brandy Surpassing Whiskey

Tracking down boozy history, especially historical spirited statistics, can be a challenging endeavor—whether it is just Wisconsin or for the rest of the country. But one thing that the *Milwaukee Journal* started surveying, by the 1940s, is the purchasing of liquor. Its twenty-fifth annual consumer analysis in 1948 revealed that 86 percent of Milwaukee-area men bought whiskey for home consumption versus 20 percent who bought brandy.

But by the 1960s, the annual *Milwaukee Journal* consumer survey was asking residents which brandies they preferred. (Coronet VSQ was frequently the number one choice, A. Gecht was often number three.) So, while this annual survey didn't track the drinking habits outside of southeast Wisconsin, it is an accountable indicator of consumption for the most populous region in the state.

Not only that, but the Distilled Spirits Institute started releasing numbers in the 1960s, revealing that Wisconsinites—not just Milwaukee-area residents—were drinking 2.3 gallons of brandy annually, or more than 40 percent of all brandy sold in the United States. In 1965, brandy made up more than one-third of total liquor sales in the state at 33.9 percent, and by 1967 it rose to 34.2 percent. Second-place Minnesota drank only a fraction of brandy, at less than 10 percent.

So, what explains this dramatic growth within two decades? In "Brandy Nippers Try to Explain Why We're High on Schnapps,"

Milwaukee Journal reporter Charlie House explored this question and refuted various theories in the June 22, 1966, issue. "The whole of the United States nips away 23.4 fifths of brandy per one hundred persons annually. But wonderful Wisconsin, the dairy state, nipped away 273.1 fifths per one hundred people! That's about twelve times greater than the national averages."

House put forth weather as an excuse, but then noted that eleven other states boast colder temperatures. He also acknowledged the ethnic makeup arguments—that Wisconsin drank so much brandy because of the state's numerous Polish, or, yes, German immigrants who brought their drinking customs to the Dairy State. He pointed out there were nine states at the time with more foreign-born Poles and six states with larger German populations than Wisconsin. Not only that, but our smaller Polish and German populations drank 273.1 fifths of brandy annually compared to New York's, who consumed only 35.8 fifths per year or an eighth of what Wisconsin folk drank. (A "fifth" is equivalent to one-fifth of a gallon; these days, that looks like a 750 ml bottle.)

Another argument House explored is that Wisconsin tastes trend toward the sweet. While House acknowledged that Wisconsinites drank more sweet, white soft drinks than many other states, he also pointed out that soda manufacturers typically stated that the reason Wisconsinites drank so much sweet soda was its ethnicity, weather, etc.

Of Access and (Marketing) Opportunities: The Less Romantic Story

So, if it's not the World's Fair, the weather, or the ethnicity of residents, why is it that we drink so much brandy? In part, House argued, it's because of access. "The real reason is that one time, years ago, when bourbon was rationed because of the war, an awful lot of brandy was shipped into Wisconsin. Because it was easier to get than whisky, people drank brandy and got to like it," he wrote. "In 1946, Christian Brothers brandy was shipped here in quantity," he continued. "About thirteen strong distributors were established to get brandy on the market significantly. They did stimulate the market."

House says he interviewed "good rememberers" like Charles W. Sand of the Wisconsin Wine and Spirits Institute who told him that we liked brandy even earlier than 1946, but House couldn't track down any reliable sales or distribution records.

This distribution theory bears a closer inspection. Another reporter, just nine years later, came to an epiphany similar to House's. Don Olesen penned "A Spirited Look at Our Brandymania" for the *Milwaukee Journal*'s Sunday magazine on December 21, 1975. Whereas House offered a humorous debunking, using some statistics and one or two quoted interviews, Olesen took a more investigative tack, interviewing more than a dozen sources. "The honest majority of my informants merely shrugged and said something like 'Well, I've been in this business thirty-seven (or six or sixteen) years and I still don't know why.' As one national brandy sales manager put it, 'It's kind of a phenomenon all by itself, like UFOs.'"

Except it isn't—and Olesen nailed down a more definitive version of House's story. Joel Goodman, who was the Christian Brothers' state manager at the time, said, "It all started out because of one factor: because in 1946, the whole state, at one time, got decent brandy."

Goodman, who had been in the liquor business since 1937, pointed out, as an exhaustive search of print materials confirmed, that Wisconsin had been drinking brandy for a long time. Before World War II, Goodman said, there was more brandy sold in the Fox River Valley than anywhere else in the state, but sales still were not booming. "Two times nothing is still nothing," he said.

But then, along came the war, and while those not serving on the front lines still thirsted after the hard stuff, there were shortages. During the war, distilleries converted whiskey production into torpedo fuel, and crops were diverted to feed soldiers. Not only that, but right after the war there was a temporary, voluntary shutdown of distilleries so that the United States government could ship large quantities of grain to feed Europeans who were rebuilding their war-torn countries. The two-month shutdown happened in 1947. "Distributors picked up all kinds of lousy rum and every kind of potato spirits, Portuguese brandy, anything they could get," Goodman said.

Numerous Wisconsin newspaper articles back this up. Several tavern owners across the state received citations or were jailed for putting bad booze into good bottles or diluting spirits, which investigating state agents discovered after testing the proofs of the liquors. Different communities, including the City of Milwaukee, had to contend with revising or rewriting city ordinances to deal with this problem in the 1940s. And at one time, state distributors, under the supervision of U.S. Customs agents in 1947, dumped 735 cases of sediment-laden Portuguese brandy into Lake Michigan on Jones Island.

Right in the midst of this rush of very bad booze, Wisconsin distributors got wind that the good Christian Brothers (Brothers of the Christian Schools Catholic religious teaching order) had a cache of aged brandy mellowing in barrels, so they ordered it in quantity. "Thus, in 1946," Goodman recalled, "about thirty thousand cases of good brandy came onto the Wisconsin market in one great gush."

Goodman's tale is backed up by a singular mention in the *Milwaukee Journal*. Under a news briefs section entitled "Whamdoodles," published on February 2, 1945, it was stated, "A state liquor monopoly in the Midwest finds itself with enough brandy on hand to float a battleship, which would be an exhilarating experience for the barnacles."

So, the story goes, when Wisconsinites had the choice between great brandy and terrible whiskey, the choice between fine brandy and rotgut rum, Wisconsinites wisely chose brandy.

A study of newspaper advertisements across the decades also supports this theory. Before this influx of Christian Brothers brandy, brandy was not listed at the top of liquor store ads, but by the 1960s it was listed at the top, before whiskey, gin, and even the then-trendy Southern Comfort.

Also, after liquor distributors got hold of that Christian Brothers' liquid gold, singular Christian Brothers advertisements started showing up in newspapers. "For complete taste satisfaction, The Christian Brothers Brandy in your favorite drink!" advises one such ad in 1947. The illustrated ad suggests using the brandy as "ideal for the 'Old

Fashioned' because of its fruity origin and flavor," and that "Many have changed exclusively to the Christian Brothers' for 'Manhattans' and the increasingly popular 'Brandy and Soda.'"

Other brandy companies also flooded the state with advertisements, and it's also quite interesting to note that in 1947 Kilian Hennessey, the sixth-generation descendant of the famed cognac producer of the same name, toured the United States after the war to promote his spirit to liquor distributors across the country. One of the stops he made was in Milwaukee. "He had been in this country ten years ago but he had never before seen the middlewest, nor so much snow, nor such cold," reported the *Milwaukee Journal* on January 9, 1947.

The more brandy Wisconsinites consumed, the more brandy was promoted.

Successful promotion and advertising campaigns might also explain why the Korbel theory gained such traction. By the 1960s, Wisconsin was completely established as a Mecca for brandy sellers, and that's when the new owner of Korbel, Adolph Heck, resurrected the winery's brandy-making operations. "In Wisconsin in particular, they did an ad in the late sixties and early seventies—since Wisconsin was a pretty value-driven state—they did an ad that went something like 'A nickel a drink more and worth it,' to upsell Korbel as a premium product," says Paul Ahvenainen, current director of winemaking at Korbel who also makes the winery's brandies. "All those things combined built the market. Wisconsin's very much a heartland state, about family, and I think a lot of our popularity is passed from one generation to another as it became a part of family gatherings."

A short article about the most popular rose in Milwaukee, aptly named the "brandy rose," mentions that brandy is Milwaukee's best-selling hard liquor, topping blended whiskey, bourbon, scotch, Canadian whiskey, vodka, gin, cordials, and rum, according to the *Milwaukee Journal* Consumer Analysis in 1965. Brandy continued to top the list of booze in this annual survey for many years.

Fruity Scofflaws: Or, Blame It on the Women

So, while this explains why brandy became our spirit of choice, this doesn't explain why we add muddled fruit and soda to our Old Fashioneds.

The addition of fruit into our Old Fashioneds is the easiest part of the Wisconsin Old Fashioned to explain. During Prohibition, quality spirits were not always easy to come by, and enterprising bartenders at speakeasies often covered up the taste of bathtub gin—or bathtub whiskey or bathtub brandy—by adding fruits and fruit juices. This phenomenon wasn't limited to Wisconsin, as it happened all over the country.

What's interesting to note is that even after Prohibition, Wisconsinites kept adding fruits and juices into drinks. Some explain that it is because residents just have a bigger sweet tooth, and they point to consumption of ice cream and sodas. But an article published in the *Milwaukee Journal* just two years after Prohibition ended offers some interesting reasons.

The story explores a bartending school "operated by a modest regard for its own products but professes now to be chiefly interested in standardizing the more or less fancy drinks of popular consumption." Tavern keepers and bartenders from across Wisconsin flocked to the three-day, temporary school set up at the Eagles club to learn from "A. I. Stone, professor of cocktails and pick-me-ups."

Stone exhorted his pupils to make sure their establishments were welcoming to women. "Wherever the ladies go the men are sure to follow," said Professor Stone in the opening session. "I mean that ladies are the most important people in modern taverns. They are responsible for the cocktail bar and the cocktail lounge. Get 'em coming your way and the rest is a cinch."

"Prof. Stone went on to illustrate the influence of ladies upon the tipples of the day. He declared that here the influence was not always happy and cited the lamentable case of the Old Fashioned cocktail, which has become a combination of fruit salad and snort, whereas its only garnishment should be a twist of lemon peel.

"The professor revealed himself a stickler for the simpler recipe whenever the customer will stand for it, but admitted to protesting pupils that if lady customers insisted on veritable banana splits with every shot it was quite all right to give it to 'em."

The professor and his assistants taught several drinks, including the Martini, the Manhattan, the Whiskey Sour, the Old Fashioned, and the Tom and Jerry, as well as several other cocktails, but exact instructions and ingredients are left out.

An earlier article that year in the *Milwaukee Journal*'s Green Sheet includes definitions for bartending slang, including the definition of a "fruit salad" as being "an Old Fashioned cocktail." Still another Green Sheet short includes an interview with a seventy-year-old bartender, who began mixing drinks in 1893 and thought the fine art of bartending was ruined by both Prohibition and women. "In those days, I knew how to mix only twelve drinks. Now, I must know how to mix more than one hundred, mostly silly, concoctions with a lot of fruit. It's an outgrowth of Prohibition and women. We old-timers don't like to see women at bars."

Whether women or men instituted the change in the Old Fashioned's garnish and flavor profile, it remains likely that Prohibition started the fruitier evolution of our drink.

TRADITIONAL WISCONSIN OLD FASHIONED

Aubrey Dodd, mixologist, Badger Liquor

1 to 3 sugar cubes
2 dashes Angostura bitters, or other bitters
1 orange wedge
1 cherry, preferably Filthy Cherries
2 oz. brandy
1 to 2 oz. lemon-lime soda, sour soda, and/or seltzer

GLASS: rocks or old fashioned
GARNISH: orange wedge and cherry on a toothpick

Place the sugar cube in the bottom of your old fashioned glass (also called a short tumbler or lowball or rocks glass). Dash the bitters on top of the cube or cubes. Then add the orange wedge and cherry, and brandy, muddling the mix together until it becomes a slushy, grainy mix—about five or six good crushes with a muddler should do it. And it's important not to muddle just the fruity part of the orange slice— muddling the peel will release its oils and add aromatics to the drink. Add ice and top with lemon-lime soda, sour soda, and/or seltzer.

For an Old Fashioned sweet, use lemon-lime soda. For an Old Fashioned sour, use a sour soda such as Squirt. For an Old Fashioned soda, use seltzer water, and for an Old Fashioned press, use half seltzer and half lemon-lime soda. Garnish with another orange wedge and cherry on a toothpick.

BRANDY OLD FASHIONED SWEET

Nathan Greenwalt, owner, Old Sugar Distillery, Madison

5 to 7 dashes Angostura bitters, or other bitters

1 maraschino cherry

1 orange wedge

1¾ oz. Brandy Station brandy, or other brandy

4 oz. lemon-lime soda

GLASS: rocks or old fashioned
GARNISH: 1 maraschino cherry and 1 orange wedge

In a glass, muddle one cherry with bitters. Add orange wedge and lightly muddle the juices from it. Pour brandy over the muddled fruit. Top with ice and lemon-lime soda. Garnish with cherry and orange.

....

THE UPSTART OLD FASHIONED

2 oz. oleo saccharum

2 to 3 dashes orange bitters, or other bitters

2 orange wedges

2 Luxardo cherries, or other cherries

2 oz. cognac or reserved brandy like Korbel VSO or
   Christian Brothers Sacred Bond, or other brandy

1 to 2 oz. club soda and/or seltzer

GLASS: rocks or old fashioned
GARNISH: orange wedge and toothpick with 2 to 3 Luxardo cherries

To make the oleo saccharum, place 4 oz. white sugar in a small bowl. Using a vegetable peeler, carefully remove the colored zest, without any white pith, from 4 oranges, 4 limes, and 4 lemons, and add the zest to the bowl. Reserve the fruit for another use or discard. Cover the bowl with plastic wrap and let sit at room temperature for at least twenty-four hours. Before using, strain the zest from the mixture, pressing to extract as much liquid as possible. Discard the zest. If the liquid isn't as much as you expected, you can add ½ cup hot water to dissolve the remaining sugar, and then strain. The oleo saccharum will not be as citrusy, but it will still be delicious.

Place the oleo saccharum, bitters, orange wedges, and cherries in a shaker. Muddle the mixture, then pour cognac or brandy on top, and shake to combine. Strain into a glass filled with ice, top with club soda or seltzer, and gently stir together. Garnish with an orange wedge and cherries.

....

UNAGED BRANDY OLD FASHIONED

Tripper Duval, Lost Whale, Milwaukee

2 oz. Torres ten-year-old brandy, or other brandy
¼ oz. turbinado simple syrup, or other simple syrup
2 dashes Bittercube Trinity Bitters, or other bitters

GLASS: rocks or old fashioned
GARNISH: cherry and orange slice

Stir all ingredients together with ice, strain into a cocktail glass, and enjoy. Garnish with a cherry and orange if desired.

Turbinado simple syrup can be made by combining equal parts turbinado sugar and hot water. Stir until sugar is completely dissolved. You can also use Sugar in the Raw or demerara sugar.

....

Nepal Old Fashioned at The Cheel

Kohler Dark Chocolate Brandy Old Fashioned
at Destination Kohler (Peter Kalleward)

NEPAL OLD FASHIONED

Drew Kassner, general manager and head mixologist,
The Cheel, Thiensville

½ oz. simple syrup
¾ oz. Amilo sour mix
1 Amarena cherry, or other cherry
1 wedge of grapefruit, ½- to 1-inch cube
1 full dropper of Bittercube Jamaican No. 1 bitters, or other bitters
1½ oz. cognac or a brandy of your choice
2 oz. seltzer

GLASS: rocks or old fashioned
GARNISH: dehydrated blood orange wheel and Amarena cherry

Muddle simple syrup, sour mix, cherry, grapefruit, and bitters together
in a rocks glass. Add ice, pour in cognac, and top with seltzer. Garnish
with dehydrated blood orange wheel and Amarena cherry. Instead of
seltzer, consider using Top Note grapefruit soda to make a delicious
sour old fashioned.

Amilo sour mix can be made by combining 1 cup fresh lemon juice,
1 cup fresh lime juice, 1 cup sugar, and 1 cup hot water. Whisk everything
together until sugar is dissolved.

. . . .

KOHLER DARK CHOCOLATE
BRANDY OLD FASHIONED

Peter Kalleward, mixologist, Destination Kohler, Kohler

2 Luxardo cherries, or other cherries
4 dashes Angostura bitters, or other bitters
splash of water, about ½ oz.
½ oz. Solerno Blood Orange Liqueur, or other orange liqueur
2 oz. Kohler Dark Chocolate Brandy, or other brandy
1 oz. club soda

Muddle cherries with Angostura bitters and a splash of water in the bottom of a glass. Add ice, then pour orange liqueur and chocolate brandy over. Gently "roll" or pour the ingredients back and forth from the original glass to another, larger glass until mixed and combined (it's like shaking, but not so violent). Strain into a rocks glass filled with ice, top with club soda, garnish with cherry and orange.

....

VASCO OLD FASHIONED, WISCO STYLE

bartending staff at Movida Restaurant, Milwaukee

2 oz. Korbel or Spanish brandy, preferably ten-year-old Torres

¾ oz. freshly squeezed lemon juice

¼ oz. chili simple syrup

1 large strawberry, cut into quarters

1 orange slice

1 dash Bittercube Trinity bitters, or other bitters

1 dash Angostura bitters, or other bitters

2 oz. seltzer

GLASS: rocks or old fashioned
GARNISH: skewered orange peel and strawberry

Place strawberry quarters and orange slice in the bottom of a stainless-steel cocktail shaker. Muddle once or twice with a muddler. Add brandy, lemon juice, and chili simple syrup to the shaker, and top with ice. Give it a good, long shake (about fifteen seconds), double-strain into a glass using a cocktail strainer and a tea strainer. Add ice, both bitters, and top with garnish.

Chili simple syrup can be made by combining 1¼ tsp. dried chili flakes, four cups hot water, and four cups sugar. Steep chili flakes for fifteen minutes, then strain.

....

Vasco Old Fashioned at Movida Restaurant (Stand Eat Drink)

BARREL-AGED BRANDY OLD FASHIONED

Tripper Duval, owner, Lost Whale, Milwaukee

80 oz. (10 cups) Torres ten-year-old brandy, or other brandy
10 oz. (1¼ cups) turbinado simple syrup, or other simple syrup
2½ oz. (2½ tbsp.) Bittercube Trinity Bitters, or other bitters
3-liter oak barrel (for aging the cocktail)

Follow barrel maker's instructions to prepare barrel for filling. Pour all ingredients into a four-liter container (like a pitcher), stir until blended. Then pour cocktail, using a funnel, into the barrel. Let the barrel rest for two weeks, rotating the barrel clockwise every two to three days. Cocktail will last for a significant amount of time, so age for taste! Enjoy.

To prepare a barrel for batching cocktails, fill the barrel with hot distilled water. Let sit in a sink for twenty-four hours so the wood will expand. This will also expose any leaks. If there are leaks, let it sit another day or two until the wood has expanded to eliminate any leaks. Drain and use.

To make the cocktail, pour 3 oz. barrel-aged mix into a glass filled with ice, stir for thirty to sixty seconds, and top with 3 oz. soda. Garnish with a cherry and orange if desired.

. . . .

The Brandy Manhattan as State Drink?

While marketing and Prohibition explain most of the evolution of our state drink, for many years, the Old Fashioned wasn't the most popular brandy drink in our state.

From the 1940s onward, liquor advertisements included specific cocktail suggestions for their various spirits. Like the earliest Christian Brothers advertisements promoting brandy Old Fashioneds and brandy and sodas, other brandy makers like Coronet and J. Bavet promoted their brandies in Stingers, Sours, and Old Fashioneds. In 1954, Henri-C Ten Star Brandy ran an advertisement admonishing, "What's Manhattan got . . . that we ain't got? Be in Style . . . Drink a Milwaukee Cocktail, like a Manhattan . . . but just different enough!," with a recipe of two parts brandy and one part sweet vermouth. Ray's Liquors of Wauwatosa even put together brandy Manhattan packages, selling brandy, vermouth, and cherries together. But if you were too lazy to mix your own brandy Manhattans, you could buy it premixed by Ph. Boilieux, too (and it was "Already Correctly Mixed"). A. Gecht and Jasmin Hill also sold brandy Manhattans and Old Fashioneds premixed.

While the most popular use of brandy today in Wisconsin is in the Old Fashioned, at one time brandy Manhattans were our mixed drink of choice. In 1975, Demedrios (Jim) Christ, state manager for Paul Masson brandy, surveyed the brandy predilections of sixty-five different bars and supper clubs across the state. "Around Wisconsin," Christ found, "the favorite mixed brandy drink is the Manhattan, followed by the old fashioned. The top drink without a mix is brandy and water, followed in order by brandy on the rocks and brandy straight."

Amy Wimmer, who is the third-generation owner of the Del-Bar in the Wisconsin Dells, says that's true. "Definitely, the brandy Manhattan was more popular," Wimmer says. "My grandparents' generation all drank brandy Manhattans, not Old Fashioneds."

Wimmer should know. Her grandparents Jim and Alice (Jim was a quarterback for the University of Wisconsin football team in the late 1920s and early 1930s) purchased the bar, so named as it was between the Dells and Baraboo, in 1943 for $500 from its original owners, who had opened it in 1938. Her father Jeff and his wife Jane took over in

1978, and Amy took it over in 2018. "We still use my grandmother's homemade sweet and sour mix recipe in our Old Fashioneds and Lemon Drop Martinis," she says.

Wisconsinites continued drinking brandy in Manhattans throughout the ensuing decades, but their mentions and promotions lessened in frequency. By 1993, according to Bill Braier, of Bill Braier's Professional Bartending School for Wisconsin, "Old Fashioned sweets are the most popular use of brandy in Wisconsin, and any bar in Wisconsin will have brandy on the rail," he noted, in a 1993 *Milwaukee Journal* story. "Other parts of the country might not even have it."

The brandy Manhattans served back then likely were a little bit different from the Manhattans, brandy or otherwise, served today, says Tripper Duval, mixologist and co-owner with Daniel Beres of the Lost Whale in Milwaukee. In fact, they were a pretty close cousin to the current standard for brandy Old Fashioneds.

"Our Manhattans used to have a little bit of that cherry juice in there," says Duval. "Realistically, many of them were probably free pouring so it was a generous serving." Bartenders, he says, probably added about a tablespoon of cherry juice right from the jar.

The brandy Manhattan may have waned in popularity because, says Doug Mackenzie, cofounder of SoulBoxer Cocktail Company in Milwaukee, it's easier to screw up than a brandy Old Fashioned. "I've tasted some f'ed up Old Fashioneds, but a brandy Manhattan's quality can be all over the board," says Mackenzie.

The problem, he says, is the quality and care of the vermouth, and as consumers have grown more sophisticated, so have their tastes. "So many bars don't refrigerate their vermouth, but the alcohol content isn't high enough, and once it's open, even if it's refrigerated, it really only has maybe a three-month shelf life."

Mackenzie and his partner Jason Neu have plans to bottle and sell a limited amount of brandy Manhattans to their Wisconsin markets annually, in the fall before the holidays.

CHERRY MANHATTAN

Jessica Hatch, bar manager, Hatch Distilling Co., Egg Harbor

2 tsp. tart cherry juice concentrate
3 drops cherry bitters
1 tbsp. honey simple syrup
2 mint leaves
2 oz. Hatch straight bourbon whiskey, or other whiskey
½ oz. sweet vermouth
2 mint leaves and lemon peel for garnish

GLASS: rocks or old fashioned
GARNISH: mint leaves and lemon peel

Gently muddle cherry juice concentrate, bitters, simple syrup, and mint leaves. Top with bourbon, sweet vermouth, and ice and stir. Garnish with mint leaves and lemon peel.

Honey simple syrup can be made by combining equal parts honey and hot water.

. . . .

A BETTER WISCONSIN BRANDY MANHATTAN

1½ oz. fine brandy or cognac
½ oz. fine sweet vermouth
¼ oz. cherry juice
1 dash orange or Angostura bitters, or other bitters

GLASS: coupe or martini
GARNISH: orange peel and Luxardo, Filthy, or other fine cherry

Place all ingredients in a mixing glass. Stir briskly until chilled. Strain into a coupe or martini glass. Peel a small slice of orange right over the glass to express oil. Drop in the twisted peel, then drop in single cherry.

. . . .

Supper Club Suppositions

Another reason for the enduring popularity of brandy—and brandy Old Fashioneds specifically—in Wisconsin is that they both go along with the enduring popularity of supper clubs. "I think they're tied together so intricately," says Wisconsin author Terese Allen. "When supper clubs started to die out elsewhere, they stayed in Wisconsin. And I think that the brandy Old Fashioned survived, in part, because we've continued to be, by far, the most supper clubbed state in the union."

Supper clubs were first invented in California—in the 1920s, by Milwaukee native Lawrence Fink, who founded Lawry's the Prime Rib in 1938 in Beverly Hills.

While supper clubs trended around the country in the 1940s, they really took off in Wisconsin like nowhere else. Part of that reason stems from the fact that during Prohibition folks headed out to rural, vacation areas to drink (though we drank everywhere). These country roadhouses evolved into dance halls, and after World War II they evolved into supper clubs.

Supper clubs became destinations in and of themselves, and fans would drive for miles just to get to their favorites (and people still do that). And that leads to another reason why supper clubs flourished—Wisconsin

Aubrey Dodd's traditional Old Fashioned

boasted the largest amount of paved rural roads in the country because our dairy farmers needed to be able to get their milk to market.

Supper clubs, says Brian West, co-owner and cofounder of Crucible Beverage Company, are also the reason why Wisconsinites garnish their drinks with everything from briny olives to pickled mushrooms. "In speculation on where the heck the idea of our weird garnishes come from is that if we were drinking our Old Fashioneds in supper clubs, supper clubs have relish trays on a lazy susan," he says. "So you're taking a sip of your Old Fashioned and then biting into something from the relish tray, the salty and the sweet are just right there, and before you know it, that becomes the norm."

Instead of throwing in a pickled mushroom, a briny olive, or a pickled Brussels sprout, Aubrey Dodd, mixologist for Badger Liquor, recommends trying a cherry that combines both the salty and the sweet: pickled cherries. "This garnish offers a complex blend of acid, salt, and sugar to any cocktail," Dodd says. "My personal favorite uses are to pair these cherries with a Martini or Manhattan, skewer some atop a Wisconsin Old Fashioned, or add them to a charcuterie board for a trendy touch."

PICKLED CHERRIES

Aubrey Dodd, mixologist for Badger Liquor

1 cup apple cider vinegar
1 cup brown sugar
2 tsp. salt
1 tsp. whole black peppercorns
1 tsp. whole coriander
½ tsp. ground ginger
¼ tsp. chili powder
¼ tsp. cayenne pepper
1 vanilla bean, sliced and scraped
5 to 6 whole cloves
16 oz. Filthy Black Cherries, or other cherries

Combine all ingredients, except Filthy Black Cherries, in saucepan over medium heat. Cook, stirring often, until all sugar is dissolved. Cover and turn heat to low. Let liquid reduce for five minutes. Add cherries to mixture, including cherry juice. Immediately remove from heat and let stand until cool. Transfer cherries into original jars or airtight containers and store refrigerated until use.

BRANDIED CHERRIES

¼ cup water
¼ cup turbinado or demerara sugar, or Sugar in the Raw
2 dashes Angostura bitters, or other bitters
½ tsp. vanilla extract
1 lb. frozen, pitted cherries, preferably from Door County, thawed
½ cup brandy

In a small saucepan, over medium-high heat, heat water, sugar, bitters, and vanilla extract, stirring until sugar is completely dissolved. Bring to a boil. Add half of the cherries, and boil for five minutes. Remove from heat, stir in remaining cherries and brandy. Let cool completely. Refrigerate, covered, for at least one day before using. Store in the refrigerator covered for up to a month.

. . . .

Dennis Getto, the late, long-time food critic for the *Milwaukee Journal Sentinel*, referred to the supper club as a "country cousin" to the urban night club, except they typically have decades of longevity. They're frequently located along highways and near resort towns, but they offer a welcoming ambiance that makes them a destination "for an entire evening, rather than as a prelude to other entertainment."

That they still endure, Allen posits, is part of the state's *Gemütlichkeit* culture. "It's all about the camaraderie and being together in and around the context of food and drink. There's a togetherness and a sociability, but it's all around the context of food and drink."

The New in Old Fashioneds

Within the last decade, craft cocktail culture has exploded, and creative Wisconsin bartenders are reinventing and reimagining the brandy Old Fashioned. Bartenders are setting hickory chips on fire to smoke glasses for cocktails; they're making syrups out of cinnamon, cloves, and even more exotic spices; and they're muddling everything from blueberries to blood oranges. Pumpkin, pisco, and spiced apple bitters are just some of the swap-ins for cherries, brandy, and Angostura. "A lot of places are putting their Old Fashioneds on tap," says Evan Hughes, who co-owns Central Standard Distillery in Milwaukee with Pat McQuillan.

"The root of fun in what we do is the guest experience," says Duval. "If you offer something that people know, but do your own kind of creative spin on it, now you've got a signature cocktail that's not going to offend anyone. And the Old Fashioned cocktail is the most popular cocktail in the world for a reason—it can literally do everything."

The brandy can be subbed with rum or any other spirit, then the sugar can be replaced with an infused sugar syrup or even maple syrup or honey. "I see a lot of maple syrup and honey because we do that better," Duval says. "And then the options for bitters are endless. It's a really fun drink to do anything you want to it, and nine times out of ten, it's going to be great."

One of West's favorite versions of the Old Fashioned that he ever developed is called the Sugar St. Clair. "I came up with this recipe when I was working with the Brew City Bombshells, a burlesque troupe," West says, adding that he met with all the performers to come up with signature cocktails for each of them for their tenth anniversary party.

"Sugar St. Clair—her style is like Betty Page meets Dita Von Teese," he says. "Her style is very vintage yet modern. To me, what's more classic than an Old Fashioned, and what's more nouveau than gin? Plus, she's a Francophile and loves everything French so I used a French gin and a French liqueur, and then brought it back to Wisconsin by using a Wisconsin supper club mix."

The Old Fashioned mix he used in his drink is the Meyer Brothers Old Fashioned Mix, which was developed by the six sons of Lenny Meyer, who owned and ran a supper club in Saint Nazians, Wisconsin, from 1962 until 1989. "His Old Fashioneds were so popular that he had to develop his own premix to keep up with the demand," West says. "Years later, as Lenny grew older and his health began to decline, his sons decided to honor his legacy by bringing his premix to market. It's everything you need to make a classic, Wisconsin-style Old Fashioned with no muddling."

Bartenders are now, finally, making Old Fashioneds with brandy distilled in Wisconsin. Several state distilleries—including Great Lakes, Central Standard, Old Sugar Distillery, Driftless Glen, and Wollersheim—all make brandies. And Kohler Company, which boasts expertise in both luxury toilets and resorts, even makes two different chocolate brandies, Kohler Dark Chocolate Brandy and a mint version. "It's been two and a half years since Kohler chocolate brandy debuted, and it's still so popular," says Peter Kalleward, mixologist for Destination Kohler.

Two companies in our state, Door County Peninsula Winery and Bittercube, make bitters. Door County Peninsula Winery makes Cherry Bluff Infusion bitters specifically for use in Old Fashioneds, while Bittercube makes a variety of bitters—including cherry bark vanilla, orange, bolivar, and trinity—that would work well in Old Fashioneds. And there's now even one company, Seaquist Orchards in Door County, that makes its own cocktail cherries, and several bars in Door County make Old Fashioneds using the locally grown cherries in place of the neon maraschino cherries.

Katie Wysocki, general manager of the former Devon Seafood + Steak, says that her Glendale restaurant's signature Wisco Old Fashioned, made with Wollersheim's apple brandy, speaks to how Wisconsinites love local twists on the state's favorite drink. "It's been a huge hit," Wysocki says. "We've been going through two cases of brandy a month."

The idea behind the drink came from Chelsea Machajewski, a server at the restaurant, and the Wisco Old Fashioned not only uses a locally made brandy or whiskey (for those who prefer whiskey) but it also replaces the soda with freshly pressed apple cider from Apple Holler. "I love apple cider in the fall, and I love Old Fashioneds, so I thought, why not combine them?" Machajewski says.

"It's a Wisconsin pride thing," adds Maggie Carpenter, a bartender at Devon. "People in Wisconsin like things made in Wisconsin, and if you can throw the word Packer into it, they like it even better."

At Movida Restaurant in Milwaukee, the staff decided to do a Spanish spin on the Old Fashioned, using Spanish brandy and a chili syrup. "We wanted to incorporate some parts of Spain with Wisconsin," says Ryan DeRosa, beverage director for Stand Eat Drink hospitality group, which owns the restaurant. "We try to make drinks a vehicle that people relate to with subtle twists that are fun."

Two different companies—SoulBoxer and Arty's Legendary

Cocktails—are bottling premixed Old Fashioneds. Arty's bottles the cocktails with sweet or sour sodas—a brandy sweet, a whiskey sour, and a whiskey sweet—while SoulBoxer bottles theirs at a higher proof without the added soda. "I think the brandy Old Fashioned should be our state cocktail," says Mackenzie, the original distiller from Great Lakes who founded SoulBoxer with mixologist Jason Neu in 2015. "We built our company on the Old Fashioned," Mackenzie says.

In 2017, SoulBoxer added a bourbon Old Fashioned to their line, and their spirits are now sold in both Illinois and Minnesota. In Wisconsin, 80 percent of their sales are brandy, but in both other states they are split evenly between brandy and bourbon. "It's funny, looking at the data from stores in Illinois, the closer you are to the border, our brandy cocktail outsells bourbon, but the further south you go, the more bourbon starts taking over," Mackenzie says.

Per capita, Wisconsin is the largest market in the country for brandy, confirms Joe Heron, founder of Copper & Kings brandy. "The brandy belt, it's Minnesota, Wisconsin, Illinois, Michigan, but the flagship state for brandy is most definitely Wisconsin," Heron says.

Nowhere is the legacy, nor the resurgence, of the Old Fashioned more evident than in the Old Fashioned itself. In 2005, this bar and restaurant opened on Capitol Square in Madison. Not only does the restaurant feature more than half a dozen different variations of the Old Fashioned cocktail but every September it hosts an Old Fashioned day, when they sell classic brandy Old Fashioneds for only a buck apiece. The bartenders, who are filed in an assembly line, make thousands of them, and there are lines out the door.

"We don't just identify with brandy, everybody identifies brandy with us," says Allen. "It's a point of pride, and it's a point of identity, is what it is. We drink brandy, therefore we are Wisconsinites, or we are Wisconsinites, therefore we drink brandy."

As Wisconsinites travel—and as restaurateurs and bartenders from Wisconsin move across the country—they've exported our Old Fashioned to other states. In fact, the humble brandy Old Fashioned is becoming a classic cocktail of note in places like Texas, California, and Kentucky. Bartenders outside of our fine state are riffing on the brandy Old Fashioned and giving it the same craft touches they'd give a Negroni or a Sazerac.

"They're elevating it," Heron says. "It's a little bit like a band that doesn't dress up but plays really great music. In Wisconsin, it's more like this is our drink, and this is what we drink, but come to Louisville, where I live, and it's quite special. We love that drink, and this is a bourbon town."

WISCO OLD FASHIONED

Katie Wysocky, general manager and mixologist,
Devon Seafood + Steak, Glendale

1 orange slice

2 cherries

1 tsp. brown sugar

5 dashes Regan's Orange bitters, or other bitters

2 oz. Wollersheim apple brandy or Wollersheim rye whiskey, or other brandy or whiskey

3 oz. fresh apple cider, preferably from Apple Holler

GLASS: rocks or old fashioned
GARNISH: dehydrated apple slice

Muddle orange, cherries, brown sugar, and bitters together in the bottom of a glass. Add brandy or rye, ice, and top with cider. Stir for thirty to sixty seconds. Garnish with a dehydrated apple slice.

For a boozier yet still apple-centric Old Fashioned, use a Wisconsin-made hard cider instead of fresh apple cider.

. . . .

GRILLED PINEAPPLE OLD FASHIONED

Michele Price, caterer and food blogger,
appetiteforentertaining.com, Hales Corners

2¼ oz. pineapple-infused rum
¾ oz. brown sugar simple syrup, or other simple syrup
5 to 7 dashes Bittercube Trinity bitters, or other bitters
2 to 3 oz. sour soda

GLASS: old fashioned or rocks
GARNISH: rum-infused pineapple slices

Fill an old fashioned glass with ice. Pour the pineapple-infused rum, the simple syrup, and the bitters on top of the ice. Stir, then top with sour soda and garnish with a slice of the rum-infused pineapple.

To make the pineapple-infused rum, put slices from a grilled pineapple in a plastic storage container. Pour half a bottle of dark rum (preferably Roaring Dan's) over the pineapple. Cover and refrigerate for at least four hours or overnight.

The easiest way to make brown sugar simple syrup is to combine equal parts brown sugar and hot water in a small saucepan and heat over medium-high heat, whisking until sugar is completely dissolved. Let cool, then use.

. . . .

Wisconsin Gin Old Fashioned at Twisted Path Distilery
(Twisted Path Distillery)

Jazz Estate Old Fashioned at The Jazz Estate (The Jazz Estate)

WISCONSIN GIN OLD FASHIONED

Brian Sammons, owner, Twisted Path Distillery, Milwaukee

2 oz. Twisted Path Gin, or other gin
¼ oz. simple syrup
1 orange slice
1 maraschino cherry
2 dashes Peychaud's bitters, or other bitters
2 oz. sweet (or sour) soda

GLASS: rocks
GARNISH: orange slice

In a glass, muddle the orange slice, maraschino cherry, simple syrup, and bitters together. Add Twisted Path Gin, ice, and top with soda. Garnish with orange slice.

. . . .

JAZZ ESTATE OLD FASHIONED

Jeff Kinder, bar manager, Jazz Estate, Milwaukee

2 oz. Woodford Reserve Bourbon, or other whiskey
½ oz. Averna Amaro Siciliano, or other amaro
½ oz. cold-brew coffee
¼ oz. Jazz Syrup, or other simple syrup
8 dashes Jazz Bitters Blend, or other bitters
orange zest

GLASS: rocks
GARNISH: orange peel

Stir all ingredients together in a mixing glass filled with ice, then strain into a rocks glass with one large ice cube, if available. Garnish with orange peel.

Cold-brew coffee can be made by combining ½ pound coarse-ground espresso beans and 1 gallon water. Soak coarse-ground beans for eighteen to twenty hours in water, then strain.

Jazz syrup can be made by combining 1 cup turbinado sugar and 1 cup white sugar in 1½ cups hot water in a small saucepan. Heat over medium-high heat, whisking until sugar is completely dissolved. Add zests of 2 lemons, 2 limes, and 2 oranges, a vanilla bean, a cinnamon stick, and a pinch of salt. Let cool, cover, and let sit for at least two hours. Strain and use.

Jazz bitters blend can be made by combining ½ oz. Angostura bitters, ½ oz. Peychaud's bitters, ½ oz. Regan's Orange bitters, and ½ oz. Copper & Kings absinthe.

....

HIBISKY OLD FASHIONED

Jessica Hatch, bar manager, Hatch Distilling Co., Egg Harbor

½ oz. hibiscus syrup

3 dashes Angostura bitters, or other bitters

orange wedge

1 to 2 Door County cocktail cherries, or other cherries

2 oz. Hatch straight bourbon whiskey, or other whiskey

4 oz. white soda

GLASS: rocks or old fashioned
GARNISH: cherries and orange wedge

Muddle hibiscus syrup and bitters with orange wedge and cherries in bottom of glass. Add whiskey, top with ice and soda. Garnish with cherries and orange wedge

Hibiscus syrup can be made by combining 2 cups water, 1 cup honey, and 10 hibiscus leaves in a saucepan over medium-low heat. Simmer for five minutes. Let cool, cover, and let sit overnight. Strain out hibiscus leaves.

....

Hibisky Old Fashioned at Hatch Distilling Co. (Kyle Edwards)

THE SUGAR ST. CLAIR

Brian West, owner, Crucible Beverage Company, Milwaukee

2 oz. Gabriel Boudier Saffron-Infused gin, or other gin
¼ oz. Gabriel Boudier Creme de Framboises, or other liqueur
¼ oz. Meyer Brothers Old Fashioned Mix, or other mix

GLASS: old fashioned or rocks
GARNISH: lemon or orange peel

Add all ingredients, with ice, to a mixing glass. Stir to chill, then strain into an old fashioned glass filled with ice. Garnish with either a lemon peel for a brighter note, or an orange peel for depth.

. . . .

OLD PASSIONS, A TRADITIONAL SORT OF OLD FASHIONED

Matt Tunnel, mixologist, Great Lakes Distillery, Milwaukee

2 oz. Kinnickinnic whiskey, or other whiskey
1 oz. Good Land orange liqueur, or other liqueur
2 dashes Angostura bitters, or other bitters

GLASS: rocks
GARNISH: orange peel

Fill rocks glass with ice. Pour whiskey and orange liqueur over ice. Add bitters, stir, and garnish with orange peel.

....

How Sweet It Is: Depends on Where You Are in Wisconsin

While you could debate whether an Old Fashioned tastes better with brandy or whiskey or sweet or sour soda, there are other, more pressing arguments to be had over making the Wisconsin Old Fashioned. Aubrey Dodd, who travels across the state of Wisconsin for Badger Liquor to teach bartending to both professionals and consumers, says bartenders get into passionate discussions, not over the booze or the soda that's added but the sugar.

Dodd says her personal preference is to use a simple syrup—sugar dissolved into water—instead of sugar cubes because the drink's texture ends up with a silkier mouthfeel, but some bartenders believe that to be anathema to the cocktail. "They believe that the cocktail should have the feel of the granulated sugar in the drink, that it's part of its charm," she says. "When you muddle the cube or cubes with the cherry, the orange, the bitters, and the brandy, you want it to be a sugary sludge."

That's actually the way the Old Fashioned restaurant and bar in Madison makes them—and the Old Fashioned cocktail-making kits they sell to customers contain sugar cubes, not regular sugar or simple syrup.

Whether to use a cube or a syrup isn't the only part of the sugar debate. It's the amount of sugar or syrup. For bars and customers in the southern half of Wisconsin, Dodd typically adds only one or at most two sugar cubes to the drink. But for anyplace north, she adds three cubes. "Whenever I make a drink in Green Bay, I always add at least a quarter-ounce more of simple syrup," she says.

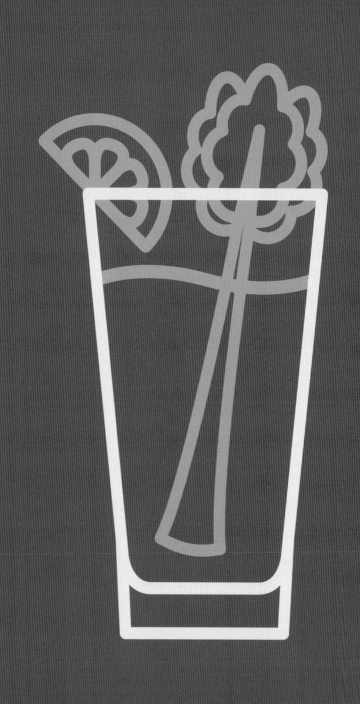

№ 2

——

BLOODY MARYS,
BEER CHASERS,
AND
RED ROBINS

OR, A BLOODY GOOD DRINK IN WISCONSIN

THE ACTUAL BLOODY MARY DRINK HAS FRENCH ROOTS, AND LIKE OH-SO-MANY CLASSIC COCKTAILS ITS ACTUAL CREATION IS AS MUDDLED AS A PROPERLY MADE MOJITO.

One of the most likely stories is that it was created by Fernand "Pete" Petiot, who worked in the 1920s at Harry's New York Bar in Paris. The story goes that he mixed tomato juice and vodka for American expats, and then he took the cocktail back with him when he moved on to the St. Regis Hotel bar in New York City after Prohibition.

While it is known that Petiot made a mean Bloody Mary while he was at the St. Regis's King Cole Bar when he took over the helm in 1934, it's unknown whether he actually mixed it or some semblance of it while he was in Paris. A cocktail book published by Harry's Bar owner Harry McElhone in 1927 seems to dispute this claim, as the book doesn't include that cocktail at all. The drink he made in New York was called the Red Snapper, and it was made with vodka, tomato juice, citrus, and spices. It's said that Petiot initially wanted to call it a Bloody Mary, but the hotel's owner (who happened to be married to a woman named Mary) was taken aback by the name. In any case, the recipe for the drink was included by the time Crosby Gaige's *Cocktail Guide and Ladies' Companion* was published in 1941.

Where things get even more muddied, er, muddled, is that there are other stories about the drink's birth. Comedian George Jessel mentioned it in a 1939 *New York Herald Tribune* piece, calling it the latest pick-me-up. Jessel claims he invented it in a Palm Beach restaurant back in 1927, saying the name came from actress Mary

Warburton, who walked in, sipped the drink, and spilled it all over her white dress, thus christening the cocktail.

Petiot later argues with this story in a 1964 *New Yorker* interview, saying, "I initiated the Bloody Mary of today. George Jessel said he created it, but it was really nothing but vodka and tomato juice when I took it over." Those additions—lemon juice, Worcestershire sauce, salt, black pepper, and cayenne pepper—make the Bloody Mary oh-so-much more than tomato juice and vodka. It's also worth noting that the Bloody Mary is a boozier variation on a nonalcoholic cocktail served in Prohibition that was simply called a tomato juice cocktail (it was often served as a first course during this time period). Later on, Tabasco sauce, horseradish sauce, and celery salt get added to the mix as well.

In any case, both vodka and Bloody Mary cocktails came into vogue in the 1940s. Around the same time, this cocktail definitely landed and took root in Wisconsin. The earliest print references to the Bloody Mary cocktail in Wisconsin came from Associated Press wire articles in the mid-1940s, describing the cocktail in New York City, as well as who was drinking it and where it was being consumed. Robert C. Ruark wrote a couple of stories in 1949 that were distributed throughout newspapers in Wisconsin, and he described it thus: "Enjoying considerable vogue right now is a nauseous blend of vodka and tomato juice, which is called a Bloody Mary and purports to cure early morning anguish without crippling or blinding the patient."

And what is perhaps the first local reference came from the *Iron County News* in Hurley on January 7, 1949, in a column entitled "This and That" by "Honest Ed." "They winced when this sophisticated lady came in on the morning of January 1 and asked for a 'Bloody

Mary.' They didn't know the old gal was suffering from a hangover and all that she wanted was a tall glass of tomato juice."

By the 1950s and 1960s, the Bloody Mary had established a foothold in Wisconsin's drinking habits; it was especially marketed to women, in print advertisements for vodka, and it was also considered a reputable hangover cure.

One of the most interesting references, though, ironically came through a nonalcoholic cocktail event for elected officials in Dane County. *Capital Times* reporter Irvin Kreisman wrote a story, published February 21, 1963, entitled "Officials Taste Them: Bravely Nonalcoholic Cocktails Feature of County Dinner." Kreisman wrote that it was "something new in public entertainment" at the Dane County Public Officials Night in the Youth Building on the Dane County Fairgrounds. "The result was as novel as the ideas," he wrote. "Some of the public officials present, especially state and city, approached the drinks rather halfheartedly, quaffed them down gingerly, then backed off as if they had seen their duty and done it."

TOMATO BUTTERMILK PICKUP

from the *Capital Times*

4 cups cold buttermilk
2 cups chilled tomato juice
salt
Tabasco, Worcestershire sauce can be added

Combine buttermilk and tomato juice and salt. Mix by shaking or with a rotary beater.

The most telling description is so very Wisconsin; it also reveals how established the Bloody Mary was: "A few of the politicians appeared to be making their first acquaintance with the new concoctions, making such natural mistakes as calling what was labeled a tomato buttermilk a 'Bloody Mary' and a lime buttermilk a 'Crème de menthe'." It's also worth mentioning that cheeses were served, with the then–Alice in Dairyland on hand to promote them.

By the 1970s, Bloody Marys were served at bars upon opening at 8 a.m., they were sometimes offered as free drinks at brunches, and there even was a *Capital Times* reporter in Madison who wrote two back-to-school stories, in both 1970 and 1971, about a group of West Side moms who celebrated the start of the school year with pitchers of Bloody Marys. There were a couple of bowling teams in Neenah named the Bloody Marys during this same time period, as well.

But just as we do the Old Fashioned differently, our Bloody Mary has developed into its own unique cocktail, something completely separate from what the rest of the country serves.

"It's a beautiful thing that the Bloody Mary has evolved to what it is today," says James "Jimmy Luv" Roeglin, president and founder of Jimmy Luv's Bloody Mary Mix. "It's the one cocktail that can get customers into a bar early and keep 'em there. And it's definitely a *When Harry Met Sally*, I'll-have-what-she's-having kind of moment whenever it's done well."

Claire Menck, PhD, chef and owner of Girlchef catering company in Milwaukee, has been mixing Bloody Marys and tinkering with her recipe ever since she started making them for the famed Ovens of Brittany restaurant in Madison back when she was nineteen years old. "I feel if you live in Wisconsin and don't have a solid Bloody Mary recipe, you have a problem," says Menck.

Menck has her basic, go-to recipe, and then she also has a fancier version she makes with a beef demiglace and a smoking gun called the Smoking Bull. "It's like drinking a campfire," she says. "It's such a lush experience."

There are two points of differentiation for a Wisconsin Bloody Mary and a Bloody Mary made anyplace else. The first is, just about every single Bloody Mary served in our state comes with its own meal on top, as its garnishes are so crazy wonderful. The second is that pretty much every single Bloody Mary here comes served with a beer chaser.

And if you, like my hairdresser, order a Bloody Mary at a theme park in Florida while on vacation and it comes with a measly little pickle and no beer chaser, you will be both disappointed and perplexed.

Nathaniel Smith, a brand ambassador for Teeling Irish Whiskey, is a bartender based out of the Twin Cities, and he knows of our state's great fondness for a well-made and well-dressed Bloody. "I once had someone order a Bloody Mary at 6 p.m.," Smith recalls. It's unusual enough for someone to order a Bloody in the early evening, but when Smith served it to him, the man's face just drooped immediately, so utterly crestfallen and sad. "He's looking at me, asking 'Where's all the stuff on it?'" Smith says, adding that he told him that at this Twin Cities establishment, Bloodies didn't come with "stuff."

"He goes 'Wait, I thought all Bloody Marys came with the stuff,'" Smith says. "He's at a fine dining restaurant not focused on brunch or

Bloody Marys so it's amazing to think that every bar he's ever been to has topped their Bloody Marys with everything they can."

Paul Ward, general manager of Ashling on the Lough in Kenosha, says his staff serves up to 200 Bloody Mary cocktails on a typical Saturday, another 150 or so on a typical Sunday, and "that doesn't include the ones we make all week long." Ashling has won the best Bloody Mary in Kenosha award for several years running, and bartenders here can go through more than twenty gallons of homemade Bloody Mary mix in a week. "We're constantly moving the mix so it's consistently fresh," he says.

They also infuse their vodkas with different vegetables. Red, green, and yellow peppers go into the mild infusion, jalapeños go into the medium infusion, and habaneros go into the spicy infusion.

At Ashling, their Bloodies are topped with a Klement's beef stick, a Mozzarella cheese stick, a pickle, an olive, a lemon wedge, a lime wedge, and a slice of bacon. "Everything's better with bacon," he says. "And the Bloody Mary itself goes into a schooner glass, which is pretty solid, large, and it's eye-popping when you see the Bloody Mary in the glass."

Incidentally, the recipe for the Bloody Mary mix is the same one that they use at both St. Brendan's Inn in Green Bay and at the County Clare in Milwaukee. At the County Clare, it's not topped with bacon, but instead with a brined red potato. Beer chasers are not only served with the cocktail, but Guinness actually gets mixed right into the Bloody Mary itself.

"There isn't really a right way or a wrong way to make a Bloody Mary," Ward says. "There's just your way. It's how you like it, and that's kind of the beauty of the Bloody. It's evolved into this cool, kind of fun phenomenon that every bar has its own take. It's become that kind of door buster prize. 'Ooh, you have to go to this bar because their Bloody Mary is made in this certain way.' I don't know of any other cocktail that does that."

Matt Anderson, owner of Matty's Bar and Grille in New Berlin, says that when a bar makes a good Bloody Mary, it's a real point of differentiation, and it's a selling point that attracts customers from a wide area.

Matty's, which won the 2018 Best Bloody Mary competition in Milwaukee, says that his staff goes through at least twenty gallons of homemade Bloody Mary mix on an average Saturday. Their Bloodies are so popular that he devised a system to serve them on tap and keep the mix both cold and properly churned. "The consistency is amazing," says Anderson.

Every table is topped with a box of seven different hot sauces so people can customize the heat in their Bloodies, and every Bloody comes with a beer chaser of the drinker's choice. Customers also get to choose between two different Marys. The Matty Mary is topped with a celery stalk, green onion, pickled asparagus, Brussels sprout, kosher dill pickle, cherry tomato, olive, pepperoncini, a jalapeño/Cheddar beef stick, and a Mozzarella cheese whip. The Ultimate Matty Mary comes in the same 25-ounce size with all of the above-mentioned toppings, plus a specialty topping of the day. Specialty toppings have included beef brisket, brats, tamales, bourbon-glazed meatballs . . . whatever the chef is thinking of that goes with a Bloody.

"They really have a wow factor," Anderson says.

The Stuff: Or, How a Milwaukee Burger Bar Changed the Way We Drink Bloodies

Back in the 1970s, some Wisconsin restaurants, resorts, and supper clubs advertised Bloody Mary bars during brunch buffets, but there's no evidence that these Bloody Mary bars likely had anything on the typical Bloody Mary served today all over the state.

Today, a typical Bloody Mary gets topped with at least five or six different toppings, minimum, and almost always, there's a beef stick and some sort of Wisconsin cheese in the mix. Many places top Bloodies with more than ten toppings, and everything from ribs to pork chops to fried mac 'n cheese to burgers to whole chickens have topped our savory brunch cocktails.

In fact, a properly made Bloody Mary in Wisconsin really should be considered a meal, not just a cocktail. And if you serve brunch, you better have a good one.

But how and when did this crazy goodness start? Although it seems like we've been making our Bloody Marys like this forever, it's actually a more recent phenomenon, and it can be traced back to one entrepreneurial tavern owner in Milwaukee.

Back in 1999, Dave Sobelman opened up a little corner tavern in the Menomonee Valley of Milwaukee, Sobelman's Pub and Grill. "It was a dive bar originally," Sobelman says. "We had homeless people drinking at the bar. But I didn't want it to be like this forever, and I was really trying to make something of this corner bar. So I focused on the food, and I tried to make it the best bar in Milwaukee."

Sobelman focused on making sure he had good burgers, but he also decided that one of the things he'd seen in bars across the state were Bloody Marys. "The Bloody Mary is such a Wisconsin thing," he says, adding that he noticed that they were served pretty much every day of the week, not just on Sundays during brunch service.

Sobelman also noticed that a Tuesday morning Bloody was different from a Sunday morning Bloody. "During the week, you'd get a pickle, an olive, and lemon, and then on the weekend they'd add a jumbo shrimp and celery," Sobelman says. "And my thinking was 'Why not put the jumbo shrimp on everyday and add the celery everyday?' And once you start thinking, you start going. I'd shop at the Jewel-Osco at the time, and I'd get some pepper cheese and jars of little corn and things like that. That went on for a few months."

As Sobelman started expanding the toppings on his Bloody Mary, he also started getting to know his neighbors better, and right next to his bar was a pickling business owned by Reinhart Lieberman, who is a third-generation pickler. Previous owners of the bar had purchased pickled pig's feet and pickled herring and the like for customers to snack on, but Sobelman didn't really want to bring those items back to the bar.

Still, he decided to go and visit his neighbor to see what he had. "That day, everything changed," Sobelman says. "I walked back in his showroom, and I saw all of his different flavors of olives and onions and mushrooms and asparagus, and it goes on and on and on. I bought everything I could."

Then, Sobelman got to thinking, what goes with pickled sausage? "Naturally cheese, this is Wisconsin, so then I went, what goes with shrimp?" Sobelman says. "A lemon, but what about something with shrimp and a lemon. How about a grape tomato, as it adds color. And things kept growing from there."

Now, that was the start of Sobelman's epic Bloody Marys, but he took it even further. On one random day in 2012—it was a Saturday, Sobelman says—he decided to put a cheeseburger on top of his Bloody Mary. So, he posted a photo of it on Facebook, and then put up the comment, "Hey guys, am I going too far?" By the end of the day, he had thousands of comments on it. "Later that night, I looked at my wife, and I said 'Wow, we're on to something.'"

Sobelman didn't stop there. He added a whole fried chicken to one (it's called the Bloody Beast), he's added a skewer of bacon-wrapped jalapeño cheese balls (it's called the Baconado), one has both the cheeseburger and the bacon-wrapped jalapeño cheese balls (the Beast), one has a burger and a Coronita topped into the Bloody (the Crown Mary), and lastly, he has a bacon-wrapped chicken with bourbon sauce (it's appropriately called the Bourbonado). Or, you could just order a plain Bloody Mary with more than a dozen toppings.

What's equally amazing is that, except for the Bloody Beast, which appropriately costs $60, and the Beast, which costs $45, the others are reasonably priced at just $9, $11, or $13.

After word got out about Sobelman's cheeseburger-topped Bloody, other bars started to spice up their own Bloody Mary toppings. This practice first spread to other bars and restaurants in Milwaukee, but now you can get extravagant Bloody Mary garnishes in every corner of Wisconsin.

Dave Sobelman not only presents his claim for starting the trend of outlandishly over-the-top toppings, but he also makes a good case that he's the one who started using the leafy hearts of celery in Bloodies.

The heart of the matter is that Sobelman started saving the hearts of celery—the leafy parts that were getting discarded in produce sections of groceries all over town. "For years, I would buy a case of celery, and through the course of the week, when I had time, I would get every celery stalk, and take the hearts out," he explains. "Hopefully, by the end of the week, I'd have one hundred to two hundred hearts with leaves on them, and I put those in a five-gallon bucket in cold water. During the week, a regular doesn't need to be impressed as such, but somebody on Sunday might be from the suburbs or out on the town, and I'd use those leafy celeries for that."

Sobelman later approached local produce companies about buying them out. "I said, 'Hey, you guys are chopping up your celery,'" he says. "You see the celery in perfect little logs in the produce section. I said 'You're throwing the good parts away.' I'm going to pay for the inside pieces they throw in the garbage. But nobody would work with me."

Soon after, though, some local produce companies started marketing the celery hearts for Bloody Marys, and then, of course, other bars started using the dramatic celery hearts to garnish their cocktails, too. "So many things people picked up that I do," Sobelman says.

The Beer Chaser

On one Las Vegas online message board, a man named Joe (really) from Wisconsin posted, "My wife loves her morning Bloody Marys when we travel. In Vegas, we have been told by several different bartenders at several different casinos, that a beer chaser is a Midwest thing, because only us Midwest people request it. Same thing happened in

Seattle, Phoenix, and Portland, Maine. Is this really true? Are we the only ones who know you need a beer chaser with a Bloody Mary?"

Yes, Joe, I think this is not just a midwestern thing; instead, it's mostly just a Wisconsin thing. Roeglin, who had recently traveled to the Twin Cities to promote his Jimmy Luv's Bloody Mary Mix, says that while he did find a couple of bars in St. Paul that offered him a beer chaser with his Bloody, the practice really tends to stay inside Wisconsin. "It's funny that crossing the border into Illinois, Minnesota, or Michigan should eliminate the concept," Roeglin says.

The beer chaser—sometimes called a *schnitt*, a snit, a sidecar, or just a chaser—is a small bottle or glass of beer that always accompanies a well-made Bloody Mary in Wisconsin.

"The chaser thing," says Corinna Todd, who owns the Red Pines Bar and Grill in Onalaska with her husband Mike. "We've lived all over the country and the world, and I was so surprised by it when we moved here. It's a cool thing, and we love to introduce it to people who are visiting."

And it's been around for, well, as long as anyone can remember. While the fabulous, fantastic garnishes for a Bloody Mary have evolved over the last decade, the beer chaser that accompanies our Bloody Mary hearkens back to an earlier time.

So early that practically everyone I interviewed on the subject—including those who have been in the business for decades—don't know of a time when Bloodies haven't been served with a beer accompaniment. "I really don't know why we do that," Roeglin says. "Just some brilliant bartender, maybe."

Jim Haertel, who owns The Best Place at the Historic Pabst Brewery and who is a beer historian in Milwaukee, admits he doesn't have an answer. "I like to think I always have a story about everything, but I'm not sure who was the first to do it or why they did it."

Haertel does say that if he doesn't serve someone a Bloody Mary with its beer chaser, people complain. "Certainly, older people expect the two to come together, and they'd be disappointed if they had to pay extra for a whole pint," he says. "What's a Bloody Mary without a beer?"

Ward says that even Wisconsinites who don't drink beer expect the chaser to come with their Bloody Mary cocktails. "I had this lady come in the other day, and before she ordered, I let her know we had a happy hour, and all tap beers were only four dollars," he says. "She says 'Oh, no, I don't do beer.' So she and her friend ordered two Bloody Marys. I made them, and I brought out one beer chaser for her friend because she was pretty adamant that she doesn't do beer. She's like 'Um, doesn't this come with a beer chaser?' I was totally confused so I brought out the beer chaser, and then the lady who does not do beer, she drank her chaser."

While some folks drink it after they finish their cocktail, and some folks drink it alongside their cocktail, it's actually meant to be poured right into your cocktail as you drink it down. Marcy Skowronski, who at 94 was perhaps the oldest working bartender not only in Wisconsin but also the world until she passed away in late 2019, said that there used to be a drink popular way, way back at the turn of the previous century, that might shed some light on this practice.

"It was called a Red Robbin, and it was basically just beer and tomato juice," said Skowronski, who used to hold court most evenings at the Holler House in Milwaukee. (The Holler House, incidentally, has the two oldest bowling lanes in the country in its basement. You

MIXED
DRINKS
High Ball   15¢
Gin Buck   15¢
Whiskey Sour   15¢
Tom Collins   15¢
Sloe Gin Fizz   15¢
Red Robbin   15¢

Marcy Skowronski (Kyle Edwards)

An old-fashioned sign advertising Gin Bucks,
Red Robbins, and more (Kyle Edwards)

have to call ahead to reserve them so they can make sure their pinsetters are on duty so you can play.)

Skowronski pointed to an old cocktail beverage sign that she inherited from her late father-in-law, "Iron Mike" Skowronski, who got it from another tavern, much older than his bar, which he opened in 1908. (No, it wasn't called Holler House back then, and yes, it remained open during Prohibition. When the feds came, he simply hid the booze in the crib of his son, who later became Marcy Skowronski's husband.)

Skowronski didn't know exactly how old that boozy sign is, just that it dates to around the turn of the previous century. What this sign points to is that we likely have been drinking our beers with tomato juice longer than we've been drinking tomato juice and vodka cocktails.

And we could speculate that we drink beer as a Bloody Mary accompaniment because, well, beer is an accompaniment to many things in Wisconsin. We have a long history of brewing in our state, we don't serve our shots with water as they do in other states (really, that's a thing elsewhere), and well, beer tastes really good when it's accompanying a Bloody Mary.

In any case, it's something that we do, and it's something that we do so well that it impresses out-of-state visitors. Plenty of travel articles suggest that visitors "act like a local" and order a beer chaser with their Bloody Mary. But to truly act like a local, you don't even need to ask for a chaser.

Perfecting Your Bloody Mary— Some Experts Weigh In

Aubrey Dodd is a mixologist for Badger Liquor, one of the oldest distributors in the state of Wisconsin, and she travels the state teaching people, both consumers and bartenders, how to make their drinks taste better.

For a Bloody Mary, she suggests you start by infusing your vodka, then make your homemade Bloody Mary mix, and then garnish it with a variety of toppings.

One of the best tricks of the bartending trade, she says, is to infuse spirits with extra flavors. For a Bloody Mary, this means vodka, and Dodd has four great recipes for infused vodkas that are fantastic in a Bloody Mary.

The basic method for infusing is to place all ingredients in a non-reactive jar. Large glass pitchers or extra-large mason jars work for this. Some people just pour the liquor out of the bottle, then put in the chopped ingredients, then return the liquor to the bottle. If you do that, you might have some liquor that won't fit back into the bottle so you'll just have to drink it. Or, start with a 3-liter bottle, remove one liter, and then put the ingredients inside the bottle.

Dodd recommends letting the ingredients and the vodka sit for three days, except in the case of jalapeños. Unless you want your vodka really spicy, you just add the jalapeños for the last few hours. Or, you could use pickled jalapeños to alleviate some of the heat.

NOW SUSHI ME, NOW YOU DON'T

1 whole ginger root, washed and sliced
1 can baby corn, strained
2 tbsp. whole black peppercorns
2 tbsp. sesame seeds
1 tbsp. wasabi peas
2 liters vodka

Place all ingredients in a nonreactive container. Refrigerate. Let sit for three days, shaking once a day. After the third day, strain out the ingredients and use the vodka.

WHERE DID MY MAN-GO?

1 large red beet, peeled and sliced
1 mango, peeled and sliced
10 radishes, sliced
1 jalapeño, sliced
2 liters vodka

Place all ingredients in a nonreactive container. Refrigerate. Let sit for three days, shaking once a day. After the third day, strain out the ingredients and use the vodka.

Gin Bloody Mary at Great Lakes Distillery (Great Lakes Distillery)

DEADLY NIGHTSHADE

1 eggplant, sliced
1 red bell pepper, sliced
1 large tomato, sliced

10 button mushrooms
1 jalapeño, sliced
2 liters vodka

Place all ingredients, except jalapeño, in a nonreactive container. Refrigerate. Let sit for three days, shaking once a day. On the third day, three to four hours before straining, add the jalapeño. After the third day, strain out the ingredients and use the vodka.

. . . .

OF THE GARDEN VARIETY

6 fresh sprigs of dill, whole
3 to 4 large carrots, chopped
5 to 6 cloves garlic, whole

1 tbsp. capers
1 large white onion, peeled and sliced
2 liters vodka

Place all ingredients in a nonreactive container. Refrigerate. Let sit for three days, shaking once a day. After the third day, strain out the ingredients and use the vodka.

. . . .

Besides infusing the vodka, you can also mix up the vodka with gin, tequila . . . or even whiskey. "We think a gin Bloody is a better Bloody," says Guy Rehorst, founder of Great Lakes Distillery in Milwaukee. "And we encourage people to try it."

Every year, Rehorst hosts a big Bloody Mary bash at the distillery's tasting room, making more than one hundred gallons of the mix, and he and his staff do try to get people to try the cocktail with gin. But they're also fine mixing up the traditional version of it as well. "Vodka is still the number one spirit in Wisconsin," Rehorst says. "It's lost some to whiskey, but it's definitely still number one."

And even with the growing demand for the Moscow Mule and its simple combination of vodka, lime juice, and ginger beer, the most popular way to drink vodka in Wisconsin remains the Bloody Mary.

INFUSED VODKA BLOODY MARY

Aubrey Dodd, mixologist, Badger Liquor

1½ to 2 oz. infused vodka
4 to 5 oz. homemade Bloody Mary mix

GLASS: tall Collins, pint, or poco
GARNISH: desired toppings and beer chaser

Shake ingredients together with ice. Pour in a glass filled with ice. Garnish with desired toppings and beer chaser.

BEST HOMEMADE BLOODY MARY MIX

1½ tbsp. salt
1½ tsp. onion powder
1½ tsp. celery salt
1½ tsp. chili powder
¾ tsp. black pepper
pinch of dried dill
1¼ tbsp. Worcestershire sauce
1¾ tbsp. Tabasco sauce
37 oz. (one extra large can) Sacramento tomato juice

Combine all dry ingredients in small bowl. In a separate, large container combine Worcestershire sauce, Tabasco sauce, and tomato juice. Slowly whisk to incorporate the dry spice mix into the tomato juice blend. Mix well until all dry ingredients have dissolved. Store refrigerated until ready to use.

THE CLASSIC BLOODY MARY

Aubrey Dodd, mixologist, Badger Liquor

1½ tsp. horseradish sauce
1 tbsp. Worcestershire sauce
1½ tsp. lemon juice
1½ tsp. Sriracha sauce

pinch of celery salt
1½ oz. vodka
5 oz. tomato juice

GLASS: tall Collins, pint, or poco
GARNISH: pickled vegetables, cheese, summer sausage, lemon wedge or wheel

Combine all ingredients into a cocktail shaker with ice. Gently roll (or pour slowly and gently) into another empty cocktail shaker or a glass. Repeat this rolling process until the drink is chilled. Strain into a tall Collins, pint, or poco glass filled with ice. Garnish with pickled veggies, cheese, summer sausage, and lemon wedge or wheel.

. . . .

THE CAJUN

Aubrey Dodd, mixologist, Badger Liquor

2 dashes Tabasco
1½ tsp. cumin powder
very generous ½ tsp. black pepper
1½ tsp. dried basil
very generous ½ tsp. garlic powder

very generous ½ tsp. onion powder
1 tbsp. lemon juice
1½ oz. vodka
5 oz. tomato juice

GLASS: tall Collins, pint, or poco
GARNISH: lemon, pickled vegetables, Andouille sausage, and shrimp

Combine all ingredients into a cocktail shaker with ice. Gently roll (or pour slowly and gently) into another empty cocktail shaker or a glass. Repeat this rolling process until the drink is chilled. Strain into a tall Collins, pint, or poco glass filled with ice. Garnish with lemon, pickled veggies, Andouille sausage, and shrimp.

. . . .

THE SMOKER

Aubrey Dodd, mixologist, Badger Liquor

1½ tsp. Worcestershire sauce

1½ tsp. barbecue sauce

2 dashes liquid smoke

1½ tsp. horseradish sauce

pinch of celery salt

1 tbsp. lemon juice

1½ oz. vodka

5 oz. tomato juice

GLASS: tall Collins, pint, or poco
GARNISH: bacon, lemon, and pickled vegetables

Combine all ingredients into a cocktail shaker with ice. Gently roll (or pour slowly and gently) into another empty cocktail shaker or a glass. Repeat this rolling process until the drink is chilled. Strain into a tall Collins, pint, or poco glass filled with ice. Garnish with bacon, lemon, and pickled veggies.

....

THE SOPHISTICATE

Aubrey Dodd, mixologist, Badger Liquor

1½ tsp. garlic powder

1½ tsp. onion powder

very generous ½ tsp. dried dill

1½ tsp. chili powder

very generous ½ tsp. cayenne pepper

very generous ½ tsp. black pepper

pinch of celery salt

1 tbsp. Worcestershire sauce

1 tbsp. lemon juice

1½ oz. vodka

5 oz. tomato juice

GLASS: tall Collins, pint, or poco
GARNISH: fresh rosemary and fresh cucumbers

Combine all ingredients into a cocktail shaker with ice. Gently roll (or pour slowly and gently) into another empty cocktail shaker or a glass. Repeat this rolling process until the drink is chilled. Strain into a tall Collins, pint, or poco glass filled with ice. Garnish with rosemary and fresh cucumbers.

....

Bloody Mary at Ashling on the Lough (Harp & Eagle LTD)

AWARD-WINNING BLOODY MARY

Paul Ward, general manager, Ashling on the Lough, Kenosha

6 oz. V8 juice

5 oz. Clamato

1 oz. pickle juice

½ oz. Worcestershire sauce

¼ oz. hot sauce

¼ oz. steak sauce

dash seasoning mix of your choice

splash of Guinness

1½ oz. seven-days-infused vodka

GLASS: schooner

GARNISH: beef stick, cheese stick, pickle, bacon slice, lemon wedge, and lime wedge

Whisk together V8 juice, Clamato, pickle juice, Worcestershire sauce, hot sauce, and steak sauce. To make the Bloody Mary, dash seasoning mix, Guinness, and vodka into your glass. Top with tomato juice mixer.

Roll mixed drink between a glass with ice and one without, pour into a schooner glass, then garnish with beef stick, cheese stick, pickle, bacon slice, lemon wedge, and lime wedge.

The able bartending staff at Ashling on the Lough infuse their vodkas for seven straight days. They have a mild infusion made with celery and green, yellow, and red peppers; a medium infusion made with jalapeño peppers; and a spicy infusion made with habanero peppers.

....

THE FREE SPIRIT

Aubrey Dodd, mixologist, Badger Liquor

1½ tsp. ground ginger
1½ tsp. ground coriander
1½ tsp. cumin powder
1½ tsp. honey

1 tbsp. spicy mustard
1½ oz. Absolut Grapefruit
5 oz. carrot juice

GLASS: tall Collins, pint, or poco
GARNISH: curried vegetables, fresh cilantro

Combine all ingredients into a cocktail shaker with ice. Gently roll (or pour slowly and gently) into another empty cocktail shaker or a glass. Repeat this rolling process until the drink is chilled. Strain into a tall Collins, pint or poco glass filled with ice. Garnish with curried vegetables and fresh cilantro.

....

A Garnish Bar

When Claire Menck is entertaining—and she knows how to throw an awesome party—she likes to set up a garnish bar.

Get a large block of ice, then chisel bowls right into the block. For the first garnish, start with cheese, glorious cheese. Spicy, flavored

Wisconsin cheeses work well—Henning's makes one flavored with red hatch chili peppers that are on the mild side, but you can also get Cheddars and Jacks flavored with jalapeños, chipotles, and habaneros. Cheese curds, which also can come in spicy, Cajun, or garlic and onion seasoning, also work well.

Then you add beef sticks or cubes or jerky or sausages. But you can also add fried chicken, oysters, cooked scallops, shrimp, prime rib cubes . . . basically any kind of meat or seafood are good things to add to your garnish bar.

And then you have to add veggies. Start with fresh celery or romaine fronds, cherry tomatoes, giant cucumber slices, fresh green onions or chives or herbs that are in season. Then you can add hearts of palm, pickles, olives, pickled okra, pickled cauliflower, brined onion pearls . . . basically any and all cooked, pickled, or fresh veggies that you think go with a Bloody Mary.

"It's really fun," Menck says. "And you can make it seasonal. For Halloween one year, I used a toy skeleton, and I filled it with garnishes. The cornichon pickles were down in the hip zone."

BLOODY MARY

Jessica Hatch, bar manager, Hatch Distilling Co., Egg Harbor

2 oz. Hatch vodka
3 to 4 oz. homemade Bloody Mary mix

GLASS: tall Collins
GARNISH: celery salt, Tejan seasoning, blue cheese–stuffed olive, pickle, and Italian calabrese pepper

Wipe rim of glass with lemon wedge, then dip in celery salt and Tejan salt seasoning (a Mexican seasoning blend), pour in ice, vodka, and Bloody Mary mix, stir together then top with blue cheese–stuffed olive, pickle, and Calabrese pepper.

BLOODY MARY MIX

32-ounce can of tomato juice, preferably Sacramento

2 bar spoons (almost ½ oz.) horseradish

2 bar spoons (almost ½ oz.) Jamaican jerk sauce

2 bar spoons (almost ½ oz.) Dijon mustard

8 shakes Worcestershire sauce

8 shakes Cholula hot sauce

⅛ cup fresh lemon juice

⅛ cup olive juice

Whisk all ingredients together. Let chill at least one hour before serving.

....

KITTY'S LOADED BLOODY MARY

Kitty O'Reillys Irish Pub, Sturgeon Bay

10 oz. tomato juice, spiced with garlic powder, garlic salt, red pepper to taste

1 dash Worcestershire sauce

1 dash raw horseradish

1 dash A1 steak sauce

splash of Guinness Stout, about 1 oz.

2 oz. vodka

GLASS: 20 oz. goblet

GARNISH: lemon, sausage stick, Renard's cheese whips, pickled asparagus, green olives, pickled mushrooms, dill pickle spear, celery salt

Pour tomato juice in a glass and season with garlic powder, garlic salt, and red pepper to taste. Then add dash of Worcestershire, raw horseradish, and A1 steak sauce. Stir, then add vodka and a splash of Guinness Stout, and stir again. Pour into a twenty-ounce goblet filled with ice, then add garnishes. Sprinkle some celery salt on top.

....

Bloody Mary at Hatch Distilling Co. (Kyle Edwards)

Kitty's Loaded Bloody Mary at Kitty O'Reillys Irish Pub
(Jstodh/DoorCounty.com)

GIN BLOODY MARY

Matt Tunnel, mixologist, Great Lakes Distillery, Milwaukee

5 oz. tomato juice
1½ oz. Rehorst Gin, or other gin
½ oz. lemon or lime juice
½ oz. pickle brine
1 tsp. Sriracha sauce

GLASS: covered jar (like an eight-ounce mason jar)
GARNISH: beef stick, cheese cube, and a pickle

Combine all ingredients in a jar with ice. Cover the jar and shake.
Remove the cover and garnish with a beef stick, a cheese cube, and
a pickle.

. . . .

BLOODY MARIA

8 oz. homemade or store-bought Bloody Mary mix
1½ to 2 oz. tequila

GLASS: tall Collins, pint, or poco
GARNISH: the sky's the limit

Combine mixer and tequila into a cocktail shaker with ice. Gently roll
(or pour slowly and gently) into another empty cocktail shaker or a
glass. Repeat this rolling process until the drink is chilled. Strain into a
tall Collins, pint, or poco glass filled with ice. Garnish as desired.

. . . .

IRISH MARY

8 oz. homemade or store-bought Bloody Mary mix
1½ to 2 oz. Irish whiskey

GLASS: tall Collins, pint, or poco
GARNISH: the sky's the limit

Combine mixer and whiskey into a cocktail shaker with ice. Gently roll
(or pour slowly and gently) into another empty cocktail shaker or a
glass. Repeat this rolling process until the drink is chilled. Strain into a
tall Collins, pint, or poco glass filled with ice. Garnish as desired.

. . . .

GIN-GER MARY

8 oz. homemade or store-bought Bloody Mary mix
1½ to 2 oz. gin

GLASS: tall Collins, pint, or poco
GARNISH: the sky's the limit

Combine mixer and gin into a cocktail shaker with ice. Gently roll (or
pour slowly and gently) into another empty cocktail shaker or a glass.
Repeat this rolling process until the drink is chilled. Strain into a tall
Collins, pint, or poco glass filled with ice. Garnish as desired.

. . . .

SMOKING BULL

J. Claire Menck, owner and caterer, Girlchef.net, Milwaukee

6 oz. fresh tomato juice
1 shake Worcestershire sauce
1 tsp. sea salt
1 oz. beef stock
2 oz. bourbon
smoking gun

GLASS: pint glass and garnish plate that balances on top
GARNISH: Swiss cheese cubes, jalapeño cheese curds, cornichon pickles, candied bacon, pickled asparagus, pickled okra, and/or slices of bratwurst

Place all ingredients (except smoking gun) into a shaker filled with ice. Shake violently for about sixty seconds. Pour drink into glass, then shoot the drink with about thirty seconds of smoke. Cover glass with garnish plate and garnishes.

To make fresh tomato juice, bring a large pot of water to a boil. Separately, prepare an ice bath. Cut a small X into the bottoms of two to four tomatoes. Drop each tomato into boiling water for just five to ten seconds. Immediately remove and then plunge each tomato into the ice bath. The skin should just slip off. Remove the core from each tomato. Use a reamer to mash the tomatoes until the juice is fully extracted. Strain through a fine mesh strainer; if you want a clear juice, strain through a cheesecloth. Season with sea salt if desired. You can freeze juice in ice cube trays. Or, if you have a juicer, you can skip the boiling water part of the process and place each tomato through the juicer, skin and all.

....

Smoking Bull (Claire Menck)

A BLOODY GOOD BLOODY MARY

J. Claire Menck, owner and caterer, Girlchef.net, Milwaukee

8 oz. tomato juice

1 oz. beef stock

1 tsp. Worcestershire sauce

1 tsp. olive brine

1 tsp. kimchee juice, or pickle brine if you don't have kimchee

⅛ tsp. freshly cracked black pepper

⅛ tsp. or 1 dash celery salt

⅛ tsp. or to taste freshly prepared horseradish

⅛ tsp. or to taste Oelek Sambal (Korean chili paste), or other hot sauce

⅛ tsp. or to taste Crystal hot sauce, or other hot sauce

2 to 3 oz. vodka

GLASS: pint

GARNISH: the sky's the limit

Place all ingredients, except vodka, in a large shaker. Shake until well combined. If you are making this base ahead of time, you can store it, refrigerated and without the ice, for up to a week before using, but for best results let them marinate for at least one day in the refrigerator.

To make cocktail, put tomato juice mixture and vodka into a shaker with ice. Shake hard for at least thirty to sixty seconds. Strain into a pint glass filled with ice. Serve with garnishes of choice.

Notes on the Rim

It's not just the mixer or the quality of vodka or the beer chaser or the garnishes that matter. The rim also matters, and a properly dressed rim can add to your Bloody Mary experience.

If you've read through the recipes, you already note that Jessica Hatch rims her glasses with a mix of celery salt and Tejano seasoning.

Celery salt alone can also rim a Bloody Mary. I've also seen bars use jerk seasoning, paprika (especially smoky Spanish paprika), Cajun seasoning, lemon pepper seasoning, salt replacement seasoning, Mexican seasoning, and other seasoning blends. One of my personal favorites is Halo del Santo, which can be ordered from halodelsanto .com. It's a finely granulated salt mixed with chiles and lime, and it's made by Scott Hackler, who, although he now lives in Texas, spent more than a few years in Wisconsin.

Another good touch to properly garnish your rim is to mix in a little bit of sugar with your salt and spices. I don't know the exact recipe that Matty's Bar and Grille in New Berlin uses for their rim, but it's got just the right amount of sweetness, spice, and saltiness to enhance a Bloody Mary.

The easiest way to rim a glass is to spread your seasonings onto a plate. Then take a wedge of lemon or lime and run it around the rim of your glass. Then, carefully dip and swirl your glass onto the plate. Voilà! You've got a perfect rim.

№ 3

—

THE
TOM AND JERRY

OR, WHY BATTER MAKES IT BETTER

VISIT A GROCERY STORE OR LIQUOR STORE PRACTICALLY ANYWHERE IN WISCONSIN AFTER THANKSGIVING AND YOU'LL FIND BATTER, USUALLY IN THE REFRIGERATED OR FROZEN SECTION.

And if you're truly from Wisconsin, you'll know that this isn't premade cake batter or pumpkin bread batter or pancake batter. It's cocktail batter. Batter that's specifically made for Tom and Jerrys.

"I always explain to people that a Tom and Jerry is Wisconsin eggnog," says Corinna Todd, who owns the Red Pines Bar & Grill in Onalaska. "I put 'Wisconsin's version of eggnog' on our menu to explain it to younger people."

"We always start the Friday after Thanksgiving," says Mark Dougherty, owner of Mark's East Side in Appleton. "That's the kickoff to the Tom and Jerry season, and we always take a picture of the first person to order a Tom and Jerry, and we put it out front. Then, we stop making them in January, when it starts to wane a bit. We make our last batch or half batch, and it ends in mid- to late January."

Dougherty's business, which has been family owned since 1967, features his father's recipe for the Tom and Jerry. "The trick is in the batter," Dougherty says. "We make it from scratch, and you have to separate the egg yolks from the egg whites, and you whip the egg whites until they're almost like a meringue. We add sugar and vanilla, and then our last, secret ingredient."

During the season, Dougherty serves thousands of Tom and Jerry cocktails. One single batch of his batter fills ten restaurant-sized plastic containers. He says that a good Tom and Jerry contains about two ounces of liquor, one ounce each of rum and brandy. "We switched

Tom and Jerry at Mark's East Side

from white rum to Captain Morgan because of the spice," he says.

And the trick to really enjoying a Tom and Jerry is not to sip it through the little straw that comes with the drink—anyone who does that immediately gets pegged as someone from out of state. "You want to get a little bit of the batter and some of the water and some of the booze," Dougherty says. "If you just suck it out of a straw, it takes your breath away [because you're just sucking out the booze]. If you sip a little bit of the batter and a little bit of the water, it's so much better."

In Appleton—as in other areas of the state—local bakeries make and sell batter by the gallon during the holiday season. Lee Dubois, whom I met at Aubrey Dodd's monthly cocktail-making class at the Palomino in Bayview, hails from the Milwaukee area, but he attended school at the University of Wisconsin–Stout, and his roommate got him a job at the Marketplace grocery store in Menomonie. While his roommate sliced meats at the deli, Dubois worked in the bakery department, and right after his start in September, his bosses got him making batter to stock up for the holidays.

"I'd use thirty-six eggs, a whole container of nutmeg, a whole container of cinnamon, a whole container of rum flavoring and huge amounts of buttercream frosting," he says. "We'd stock it in the bakery section, but I also had to stock it in the alcohol section, too. By the end of the Christmas season, I didn't even want to look at a Tom and Jerry."

The Tom and Jerry is a very old cocktail. And while trendy beverage magazines and East Coast newspapers have occasionally run "revival" stories about this warm holiday cocktail to introduce it to folks who've never tried this dairy deliciousness, we in Wisconsin know better. In fact, while eggnog fortified with rum may have edged out the Tom and Jerry cocktail in the rest of the country, the Tom and Jerry has stood the test of time here. It has never had to be revived because it simply never went away.

The Tom and Jerry became a thing in the late nineteenth and early twentieth centuries. Like practically every other cocktail, its exact origin is a bit fuzzy. There are two dueling, oft-quoted tales, plus a third (and more likely) creation story. The first one says that British journalist Pierce Egan created the cocktail to publicize his book *Life in London: Or, The Day and Night Scenes of Jerry Hawthorn, Esq., and His Elegant Friend Corinthian Tom.*

"Professor" Jerry Thomas, who published the very first cocktail book in 1862, did include a recipe for the Tom and Jerry in it, and in several interviews he promoted himself as the creator of the cocktail. In an 1880 interview with a reporter named Alan Dale (a story also retold in his *New York Times* obituary), Thomas says, "I named the drink after myself, kinder familiarly: I had two small white mice in those days, one of them I called Tom and the other Jerry, so I combined the abbreviations in the drink, as Jeremiah P. Thomas would have sounded rather heavy, and that wouldn't have done for a beverage." This story was also repeated on page 4 of the January 16, 1886, edition of the *Milwaukee Journal,* under a headline "Poor Tom and Jerry." The *Milwaukee Sentinel* repeated the same story it its edition that day, too.

David Wondrich debunks this story in his book *Imbibe! From Absinthe Cocktail to Whiskey Smash.* Wondrich discovered a quite interesting story he found in the March 20, 1827, issue of the *Salem Gazette* (which is three years before Thomas was born). "At the police court in Boston, last week, a lad about thirteen years of age was tried for stealing a watch, and acquitted. In the course of the trial, it appeared that the prosecutor [the plaintiff] sold to the lad, under the name of 'Tom and Jerry,' a composition of saleratus (baking soda), eggs, sugar, nutmeg, ginger, allspice and rum. A female witness testified that the boy . . . appeared to be perfectly deranged, probably in consequence of the 'hell-broth' that he had been drinking."

Wondrich emphasizes that he found dozens of references to the Tom and Jerry drink in the 1830s and 1840s from New England sources, and since Thomas himself learned his craft in New England—in New Haven, Connecticut, to be exact—he likely learned how to properly make the drink there, right in the heart of the original Tom and Jerry country.

According to Wondrich, the drink itself rose in popularity after the Civil War. Saloons typically started serving it in October or November, and they kept serving it until temperatures warmed up in spring.

In the 1870s, china companies started making actual Tom and Jerry bowl and cup sets, but in the early twentieth century the cocktail's popularity waned in many areas of the country. So much so, that the New York *Sun* reported in 1902 that it "seems to have vanished as absolutely as the dodo." Wondrich says that the drink really fell off after Prohibition, but he also mentioned that it survived in places, and is still served around the holidays in the "Upper Midwest."

Well, he's right about that—it's still served here, in the Upper Midwest of Wisconsin. It's also served in Michigan and Minnesota, but like both the Bloody Mary and the brandy Old Fashioned, any tavern here worth its pickled eggs or cheese curds knows how to make a Tom and Jerry.

In tracing the drink's history in Wisconsin, the earliest references I found came in the 1880s. Likely it was served earlier than that, but like most trends of food and beverages today, Wisconsin isn't the earliest adopter but once we come upon something we like, we stick with it.

Those Tom and Jerry bowl and cup sets might have fallen out of fashion on the East Coast in the late nineteenth century, but they were still heavily advertised here in the early twentieth century. Some advertisements for Tom and Jerry mugs ran in the *Milwaukee Journal* in 1903. "Good Cheer for the New Year, More than 200 Styles at Amazingly Low Prices," promoted an ad for Barretts store.

But as in the rest of the country it was a seasonal drink. The *Milwaukee Journal* on October 24, 1887, under a section on page 2 called "Philosophy of the Street," reported that "There will soon be a market for over-ripe eggs; the Tom and Jerry season is approaching."

We drank it before Prohibition. We drank it during Prohibition. And we definitely have continued to drink it since Prohibition. I think it's quite telling that several winter Prohibition stories mention the Tom and Jerry by name. The *Milwaukee Journal* ran a story on January 18, 1929, entitled "Doc's Saloon Raided by U.S.": "Doc O'Donnell's place at 830 Clybourn St. was raided. Tom and Jerry was the featured drink at Doc's and a large bowl of the warming concoction was usually on the back bar. The bowl and mugs to match were relics of the pre-Volstead days."

It's also quite telling that the *Milwaukee Sentinel* published an article on December 30, 1932, exploring the prices for cocktails that readers could enjoy as part of their New Year's Eve celebrations—mind you, this is almost a year before Prohibition officially ended. "Despite recent activity of the prohibition department, Milwaukeeans bent on bringing in the baby New Year amid high wassail Saturday night will find there are reasonable supplies of the forbidden beverages available and priced to fit any man's pocketbook."

That same article pointed out that a Tom and Jerry would cost 50 cents, but that there was a shortage of Charleston and Jamaica rums, which are "the true necessaries for a first rate Tom and Jerry." A suitable substitution, however, was "a mixture of Bacardi and cut whisky," as it makes a "palatable synthetic Tom and Jerry at 50 cents the copy."

It was a New Year's tradition that continued long after Prohibition, as liquor stores advertised rum "for that New Year's Tom & Jerry" in many December newspapers. Two years in a row, in 1948 and 1949, the *Milwaukee Journal*'s food section ran dueling recipes for making Tom and Jerry cocktails at home. In 1948, the newspaper published Mrs. Karl Ratzch's recipe, as she was "long known for her delicious drinks." Since Mader's German restaurant was a competitor of Ratzch's, I'm guessing Gustave Mader complained, and the next year, his Tom and Jerry recipe was published. Mrs. Ratzch's actual cocktail was boozier, with a half-ounce more booze, but Gustave's added rum to the batter.

MRS. KARL RATZCH'S TOM AND JERRY RECIPE

from the *Milwaukee Journal*, 1948

12 cold eggs
3 cups granulated sugar
½ cup powdered sugar
24 oz. brandy
12 oz. dark Jamaica rum

To make the batter, whip egg whites until stiff, gradually adding granulated sugar and powdered sugar. An electric beater is best at low speed. Whip yolks separately until frothy. Fold beaten whites and yolks together, and keep in a cold place until used. Place one serving of batter into each Tom and Jerry cup, add one ounce of brandy and half-ounce of rum in each cup. Fill with boiling water until batter comes to the top. Sprinkle with grated nutmeg or allspice.

....

GUSTAVE G. MADER'S TOM AND JERRY RECIPE

from the *Milwaukee Journal*, 1949

12 fresh eggs, separated and cold
1½ lbs. sugar
2 oz. Jamaica-type rum
½ tsp. ground cloves

Beat whites to a stiff froth. Beat yolks separately, adding sugar slowly. Add rum and cloves. Use the electric mixer and beat until quite stiff. Fold the beaten whites into the yolks. Makes enough batter for 25 cocktails.

....

John Dye, who owns Bryant's, At Random, and The Jazz Estate in Milwaukee, says he tried to purchase Mrs. Ratzch's copper Tom and Jerry bowl for Bryant's, but he was outbid at auction. "It went up to several hundred dollars," Dye says. "Obviously, it meant more to somebody else."

By the 1960s, dieters were warned to eliminate Tom and Jerry cocktails if they didn't want to gain weight over the holiday season, and eggnog, made commercially by dairies starting in the 1930s, grew in popularity by the 1960s, edging out Tom and Jerry cocktails in many places around the country.

But the Tom and Jerry never got edged out here in Wisconsin. Dye says the popularity of the Tom and Jerry in Wisconsin makes sense. "Winters are long here," he says. "A Tom and Jerry, when it's properly made, is a fun drink. It has those elements of Wisconsin (over-the-top, sweet excess), and you add warmth to it. It's just so Wisconsin."

At Bryant's, Dye opens up a second room during the winter season just for Tom and Jerry serving, and in 2017 Bryant's finally had its own mugs printed. At Bryant's, the Tom and Jerry is served the right way—the mugs are warmed, the milk is warmed, and the booze is warmed. "Absolutely, that's critical," Dye says. "Otherwise, the drink cools down right away. We keep the booze in hot water. We just want to keep it warm—we're not talking about a lot of hotness going in. The main thing is if you have cold alcohol in a cold mug, and then you add a few ounces of something hot, the chances of the drink getting above lukewarm isn't good."

Dye doesn't recommend putting the booze on the stove to warm—that's an explosion waiting to happen. Instead, a pot of hot water, a water bath, or bain marie for the booze is the way to go.

Dougherty says that warming the booze isn't necessary, but warming the mugs—that's the only way to go if you want to keep the drink toasty and warm.

While the original batter recipes for Tom and Jerrys called only for eggs and sugar, in Wisconsin, Dye says, folks often add milk, cream, butter, or even melted ice cream.

The original batter recipes also usually just started out as eggs and sugar, but different families and different bars added in vanilla extract, some booze (usually rum and/or brandy) to the batter, and spices, including cinnamon, nutmeg, allspice, and cloves. But to finish and serve the cocktail, usually it was nutmeg that was grated over the top.

In any case, a good Tom and Jerry here in Wisconsin is like a well-made Bloody Mary—it's over-the-top goodness.

BASIC TOM AND JERRY

BATTER

4 eggs, separated
1 cup powdered sugar
½ tsp. cream of tartar
1 tsp. vanilla extract

Whip egg whites with cream of tartar until stiff peaks form. Gradually add ¾ cup powdered sugar and vanilla extract. In a separate bowl, whip egg yolks with remaining sugar. Fold egg yolk mixture into egg whites. Refrigerate until ready to use. Makes enough for about eight cocktails.

COCKTAIL

½ cup batter
1 oz. brandy
1 oz. rum
4 to 5 oz. hot milk

GLASS: mug
GARNISH: ⅛ to ¼ tsp. grated nutmeg

Heat milk until almost but not quite scalded. While milk is heating, warm up a mug with hot water, then discard the water. Pour brandy and rum into the bottom of the mug, add batter, then pour warm milk on top. Grate nutmeg as garnish.

A MODERN TOM AND JERRY

Aubrey Dodd, mixologist, Badger Liquor

BATTER

4 whole eggs

¾ cup white sugar

½ tsp. ground nutmeg

¼ tsp. ground cinnamon

1 vanilla bean, split and scraped

6 oz. Goslings dark rum, or other dark rum

2 cups heavy cream

To make the batter, mix eggs alone in blender on medium for about thirty seconds. Add sugar and blend for thirty more seconds. Add all other batter ingredients and blend for approximately twenty more seconds or until thoroughly mixed. Transfer to airtight container and refrigerate until ready for use.

This batter recipe makes approximately 20 servings and is stable if kept refrigerated for up to three weeks due to the high alcohol content. Shake well before each use as spices may settle.

COCKTAIL

2 oz. Tom and Jerry Batter

1½ oz. Central Standard North 40 Brandy, or other brandy

1 oz. Rishi Masala chai concentrate, or other chai concentrate

3 oz. whole milk

GLASS: ten-ounce mug

GARNISH: grated nutmeg, allspice, or cloves

Combine chai concentrate and milk in saucepan over medium heat, stirring often, until heated through. Add batter, brandy, and hot chai and milk mixture to a mug. Stir gently to combine ingredients. Heat your mug before making this cocktail by rinsing it with boiling water. This will help warm the batter and keep your drink pleasantly toasty as you sip. Garnish with grated nutmeg, allspice, or cloves, as desired.

If you love the chai flavor of this cocktail and want to up the chai ante, you can follow the recipe in chapter 4 for the Baaree Alexander to infuse the brandy with chai tea.

TOM AND JERRY

from Dairy Farmers of Wisconsin

BATTER

1 cup Wisconsin Mascarpone cheese

3 cups powdered sugar

6 eggs, separated (preferably pasteurized or from a local source you trust)

½ tsp. vanilla extract

½ tsp. ground nutmeg

¼ tsp. ground cloves

¼ tsp. ground allspice

¼ tsp. sea salt

1½ tsp. cream of tartar (use only if using pasteurized eggs)

To make batter, in a large bowl mix Mascarpone and powdered sugar until combined. Set aside. In a medium-sized mixer bowl, beat egg yolks until slightly thickened and pale yellow, about four minutes. Add vanilla, nutmeg, cloves, and allspice, stir to incorporate. Stir yolk mixture into Mascarpone mixture until well blended. Set aside.

In a large glass or metal bowl, beat egg whites, salt, and cream of tartar until the egg whites form sharp peaks that hold their shape when lifted with the beater or whisk. Gently fold egg whites into Mascarpone mixture, until well combined. Batter can be used immediately or stored in a tightly sealed container and frozen for up to two weeks.

COCKTAIL

1½ quarts (6 cups) milk

12 oz. rum

12 oz. brandy

GLASS: mug

GARNISH: freshly grated nutmeg

To serve, heat milk in a heavy pot over medium-low heat until hot but not scalded, about five to ten minutes. To make each cocktail, place 1 heaping tablespoon of batter in a mug, pour 4 oz. of hot milk, 1 oz. rum, and 1 oz. brandy. Grate fresh nutmeg on top for garnish. Makes twelve servings.

Tom and Jerry and other warm cocktails (Dairy Farmers of Wisconsin)

Tom and Jerry at Great Lakes Distillery (Great Lakes Distillery)

TOM AND JERRY WITH A FRUITY TWIST

Matt Tunnel, mixologist, Great Lakes Distillery, Milwaukee

BATTER

6 eggs, separated

1 lb. white sugar

pinch of allspice (about ⅛ tsp.)

pinch of cinnamon (about ⅛ tsp.)

pinch of ground cloves (about ⅛ tsp.)

pinch of nutmeg (about ⅛ tsp.)

2 tsp. vanilla extract

1 tsp. almond extract

Combine sugar, spices, extracts, and egg yolks in a bowl and beat until well mixed. In a separate bowl, beat egg whites until they form stiff peaks, then, working in thirds, gently fold the egg whites into the egg yolk mixture. Try to keep it fluffy. Cover and store in the freezer until ready to use.

COCKTAIL

1 oz. Great Lakes Plum Brandy, or other brandy

1 oz. Good Land Door County Cherry Liqueur, or other cherry liqueur

2 tbsp. Tom and Jerry batter

4 oz. hot milk

GLASS: mug

GARNISH: grated nutmeg

Pour plum brandy and cherry liqueur in a warmed mug. Add batter and then pour in hot milk and stir. Garnish with nutmeg.

. . . .

SLIGHTLY GUSSIED UP TOM AND JERRY

BATTER

2 large or extra large eggs, separated

¼ tsp. cream of tartar

½ cup powdered sugar

1 tbsp. dark or spiced rum or brandy

1 tsp. vanilla extract

¼ tsp. cinnamon

⅛ tsp. nutmeg

⅛ tsp. allspice

⅛ tsp. ground cloves

1 dash bitters

In a mixer, whip egg whites with cream of tartar until stiff peaks form. Gradually add all but 2 tbsp. of sugar into the whites. In a separate bowl, whisk egg yolks until slightly frothy, then whisk in the remaining sugar, the liquor, the vanilla extract, the spices, and the bitters. Fold a little bit of the egg white mixture into the egg yolk mixture, then gently fold the egg yolk mixture into the egg white mixture. Makes 1¼ to 1½ cups of batter. Makes enough batter for about six to eight cocktails, less if you like more batter in your cocktails.

You can also add 2 to 5 tbsp. softened unsalted butter. You would add it, 1 tbsp. at a time, to the egg whites after you've added the sugar. This adds a richness to the batter, but what you gain in richness, you lose in elevated texture, as the batter becomes thinner.

SLIGHTLY GUSSIED UP COCKTAIL

1 oz. brandy

1 oz. spiced rum or dark rum

2 tbsp. batter

3 to 4 oz. milk or water, heated

1 dash bitters

GLASS: mug

GARNISH: freshly grated nutmeg or cinnamon

Heat mug. Pour booze into bottom of mug, top with batter, pour in hot liquid, then dust with nutmeg or cinnamon and add a dash of bitters if you desire.

SLIGHTLY GUSSIED UP CHOCOLATE TOM AND JERRY COCKTAIL

2 tbsp. unsweetened cocoa powder

1 oz. rum, divided

4 to 6 oz. milk

1 oz. brandy

2 to 3 tbsp. batter

GLASS: mug

GARNISH: freshly grated chocolate

Whisk cocoa powder with ½ oz. rum and pour into mug with milk. Warm in microwave for about sixty seconds, pour in brandy and the remaining rum, and add batter. Top with grated chocolate.

....

Notes on Nogs

While we serve up more Tom and Jerry cocktails than practically any-place else on the planet, we also serve up some good eggnogs, too. And I'm not talking about the fake noggy stuff you get in a carton from the grocery store just spiced up with brandy, rum, and nutmeg.

A good nog starts out just like a good Tom and Jerry—with a home-made batter. Katie Wysocki, general manager for Devon Seafood + Steak restaurant in Glendale, makes hundreds of gallons of eggnog, and customers buy it from her for their own parties at home. "They're crazy about it," Wysocki says. "They can't get enough of it."

Though Wysocki's recipe is for parties, Brian Sammons, owner of Twisted Path Distillery, has a great nog recipe that is easy to make for just one or two cocktails, and his recipe uses his chai liqueur. Sammons makes his chai liqueur using his wife Laura Singleton's homemade chai recipe. "It blew my mind," Sammons says. It's also, he says, quite good with just vanilla ice cream.

DEVON NOG

Katie Wysocki, general manager, Devon Seafood + Steak, Glendale

½ cup egg yolks
1 cup sugar
2 cups whole milk
1 cup heavy cream
1 tbsp. vanilla extract

1 tsp. nutmeg
1½ cups Wollersheim brandy,
  or another brandy
¾ cup egg whites

Beat together egg yolks and sugar until fluffy. Whisk in milk, heavy cream, vanilla extract, and nutmeg. Whisk in brandy. Refrigerate for one hour. Whip egg whites until fluffy enough to hold a curl if the beater is turned upside down. Fold egg whites into egg yolk, milk, and brandy mixture.

. . . .

CHAI NOG

Brian Sammons, Twisted Path Distillery, Milwaukee

1½ oz. Twisted Path Chai Liqueur
¾ oz. simple syrup
½ oz. heavy whipping cream
1 whole egg
1 dash Angostura bitters, or other bitters

In a cocktail shaker, combine Twisted Path Chai Liqueur, simple syrup, heavy whipping cream, and ice. Shake. Strain the cocktail into one-half of the shaking tin and discard the ice from the other half. Add 1 whole egg, then shake vigorously for thirty seconds. Pour cocktail into glass, topping with a dash of Angostura bitters.

. . . .

Chai Nog (Twisted Path Distillery)

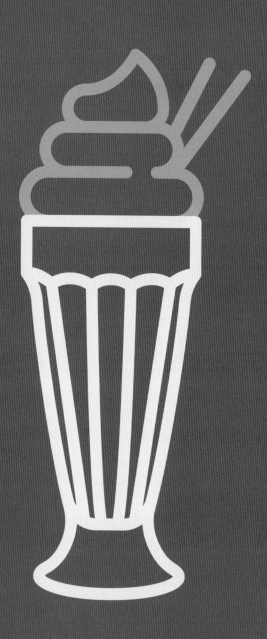

№ 4

BANSHEES, PINK SQUIRRELS, AND OTHER WILD CREATURES

OR, THE ICE CREAM DRINKS OF WISCONSIN

IF YOU ORDER A BRANDY ALEXANDER OR A GRASSHOPPER IN MOST PARTS OF THE COUNTRY, YOU'LL GET A LOVELY, CREAMY DRINK, MADE WITH HEAVY CREAM OR HALF-AND-HALF. HERE, THESE DRINKS AREN'T SO MUCH DRINKS AS THEY ARE DECADENCE EMBODIED. IN WISCONSIN, IF YOU ORDER A BRANDY ALEXANDER OR A GRASSHOPPER, YOU'LL GET A DESSERT, OFTEN TOPPED WITH WHIPPED CREAM, SOMETIMES TOPPED WITH CHOCOLATE PIECES, BUT ALMOST ALWAYS MADE WITH ICE CREAM.

In other parts of the country, booze and ice cream together is called a boozy milkshake. Though some Wisconsin bars and restaurants now put "boozy milkshakes" on their menus, most places still call them ice cream drinks. Or, rather, just drinks. And any supper club worth its relish tray serves up hundreds of them on a Saturday evening.

But how did Wisconsin end up combining booze and ice cream together—and combining them in such large quantities?

Part of the answer to this question is just that we are America's Dairyland, and though we do produce plenty of heavy cream and half-and-half, we produce a lot more ice cream and frozen custard, and we've always produced a lot of this dairy deliciousness. Two Rivers, Wisconsin, claims to be the birthplace of the ice cream sundae, and our dairy industry has always promoted ice cream.

"The whole kind of dairy tradition—custard and ice cream—is so strong, it kind of makes sense that they were paired together with cocktails," says John Dye, owner of three historic bars in Milwaukee, Bryant's Cocktail Lounge, At Random, and The Jazz Estate. "I've always been of the opinion that in Wisconsin, we can take anything that's bad for you and make it worse."

But the other part of this equation lies within the manufacturing history of our state.

A Blended History

Besides the strong dairy tradition, we also have a strong manufacturing tradition. In fact, blenders were invented in Racine, Wisconsin. The first blender (as we know it) was invented by a Polish immigrant, Stephen Poplawski, who was hired by the Arnold Electric Co. to develop an automatic malted milk mixer—Racine also happens to be the home of Horlick's Malted Milk—and in 1922, Poplawski received a patent "for the first mixer of my design having an agitating element mounted in a base and adapted to be drivingly connected with the agitator in the cup when the cup was placed in a recess in the top of the base." Poplawski eventually went on to form his own company, Stephens Electric Co. In 1940, he patented a home mixer; in 1946, he sold his business to the John Oster Manufacturing Co., which renamed this mixer the Osterizer.

But that's just one of the blenders with Wisconsin roots. Another forerunner of the blender was also invented in Wisconsin, and this is where the history gets a little bit, ah, blended. Stephen Beach and Louis Hamilton had worked at U.S. Standard Electric Company, and then worked together at the same Arnold Electric Company where Poplawski worked, but they worked at Arnold in the early twentieth

Grasshopper, Brandy Alexander, and Pink Squirrel at the Del-Bar (Del-Bar)

century. There, they improved upon the first lightweight, high-speed universal motor. But when the company was sold, they joined forces with Fred Osius in 1910 to form the Hamilton Beach company, also based in Racine. Beach was the mechanical guy, Hamilton was the business pro, and Osius drove sales and financed their operation.

Here, one of the very first inventions they promoted was the Cyclone Drinks Mixer in 1911. "Cocktail mixers, as far as I can tell, were invented to replace shaking," Dye says. "They basically have shaker tins attached to the base. It looks like they made flips and stuff in there."

Dye owns an antique blender that likely dates back to this time period (he found it at an estate sale—not in the bar). "The blades on these original ones were these little paddles," Dye says. "They didn't cut ice or ingredients, they mixed things."

And mixing is a bit different than blending and chopping, which good blenders do.

Now, obviously, the Cyclone Drink Mixer ended up not doing any legal cocktail mixing after Prohibition, but these guys at Hamilton Beach kept working on their own blender and blender-like devices, but to really move things along they needed some additional financing. So Osius, the money guy, approached big-band leader Fred Waring, of Fred Waring and His Pennsylvanians. The story goes that Osius introduced the idea to Waring backstage one night after Waring's radio show. Waring himself was a former engineering student and liked gadgets. This blender idea caught his interest for two reasons: one, it would help him liquefy the fruits and veggies his doctor prescribed for his ulcer, and two, it could mix drinks. By 1937, it became known as the Waring Blender, and with Waring promoting the heck out of it—and plugging its use for cocktails—the rest is blender history.

For a long time, blenders were manufactured in Wisconsin by both the Oster and Hamilton Beach companies, and they were obviously sold to plenty of homes, bars, and restaurants within the state. Having them on hand could be a reason why we enjoy ice cream drinks—because the bars and restaurants were outfitted to do so.

Creamy Drinks Come of Age

The original creamy drink was simply called an Alexander, and it was made with gin, crème de cacao, and cream. Like any good cocktail, there are quite a few legends of how it came to be, but the first time it showed up in a recipe book was in Hugo Enslin's *Recipes for Mixed Drinks* in 1916. Bartenders started replacing the gin with other elixirs, including brandy, and Prohibition didn't exactly stop folks from drinking the creamy, sweet stuff. Post-Prohibition, and by 1937, the drink showed up in Stanley Clisby's *Famous New York Drinks and How to Mix 'Em*. In Clisby's volume, the drink (which he spells "Alexandre") calls for a pony (or shot) each of gin, crème de cacao, cream, and one egg white.

The earliest print reference in Wisconsin I could find to the Alexander cocktail is an advertisement for Du Bouchett in the April 6, 1934, edition of the *Milwaukee Journal*. The ad calls for one-third Du Bouchett crème de cacao, one-third Du Bouchett gin, and one-third cream, instructing to shake with ice and serve. In 1942, a bartender named Edward J. Klun got arrested for drunk driving after he jumped into a taxi and drove away with it. His lawyer, in pleading to get his bartending license restored, said to the Milwaukee Common Council, "My client is interested in chemistry. He met another bartender, and they decided to try a little experiment with a concoction called an 'Alexander cocktail.' It turned out to be 'Alexander the Conqueror.'" The council accepted Klun's lawyer's excuse and reinstated his tavern license over police objections.

In the 1930s, brandy versions of the Alexander also started showing up in cocktail books, and they definitely started showing up in Wisconsin bars and supper clubs. By the 1950s and 1960s, the Alexander cocktail had really morphed into the Brandy Alexander cocktail. (Even some French poodles in Wisconsin were christened with the drink's name by this time!)

BRANDY ALEXANDER

Amy Wimmer, owner, The Del-Bar, Wisconsin Dells

½ oz. dark crème de cacao
½ oz. brandy
3 scoops vanilla ice cream

GLASS: poco, hurricane, or rocks
GARNISH: homemade whipped cream and nutmeg

Pour crème de cacao and brandy into the bottom of a blender. Top with ice cream. Blend until creamy and smooth. Pour into glass, top with homemade whipped cream and nutmeg.

....

BAAREE ALEXANDER

Drew Kassner, general manager and head mixologist, The Cheel, Thiensville

1½ oz. chai-infused brandy, preferably Central Standard Distillery's North 40
1½ oz. dark crème de cacao
3 big scoops of vanilla ice cream, preferably Cedar Crest of Sassy Cow,
    left to sit at room temperature for about three to five minutes to soften
1 tbsp. heavy cream

GLASS: pint
GARNISH: Amaretto whipped cream, cinnamon, cinnamon sticks

Place brandy and dark crème de cacao into blender. Top with ice cream and heavy cream. Blend until smooth, thirty to sixty seconds. Top with Amaretto whipped cream, cinnamon, and cinnamon sticks.

Chai-infused brandy can be made by combining 3 tbsp. Rishi chai tea (or other chai tea) and one 750 ml bottle brandy (preferably Central Standard Distillery's North 40). Let sit for two hours, then strain and use. While Barkha Daily makes her own chai tea for The Cheel, she says that Rishi is a fantastic substitute for people who don't have mothers sending them spices direct from Nepal. "The only difference from

Baaree Alexander at The Cheel

making this at home is that the flavors are a little more robust at the restaurant," Daily says. "But it's a very similar flavor profile, and it's much easier for someone to make at home."

Amaretto whipped cream can be made by whipping together 1 pint heavy cream (unsweetened, no additives), 2 tbsp. sugar, and 1½ to 2 oz. Amaretto (or other almond liqueur).

....

The Grasshopper cocktail was never made with gin, and it's about as old as the Alexander. Most likely, the Grasshopper was invented in New Orleans in 1919 at Tujague's. Louisiana lore has it that it was invented by owner Philibert Guichet, who first created it for a New York City cocktail competition, making it with equal parts crème de menthe, crème de cacao, and cream. This drink, while served illegally during Prohibition, migrated outside of New Orleans, and it took firm root in Wisconsin along with the Brandy Alexander.

GRASSHOPPER

Amy Wimmer, owner, The Del-Bar, Wisconsin Dells

½ oz. green crème de menthe
½ oz. white crème de cacao
3 scoops vanilla ice cream

GLASS: poco, hurricane, or rocks
GARNISH: homemade whipped cream and drizzle of crème de menthe

Pour crème de menthe and crème de cacao into the bottom of a
blender. Top with ice cream. Blend until creamy and smooth. Pour
into glass, top with homemade whipped cream, then drizzle crème
de menthe on top.

. . . .

GRASSHOPPER KRINGLE

Kringle Cream mixologists

2 oz. Kringle Cream liqueur
1 oz. green crème de menthe
1 oz. white crème de cacao

GLASS: martini or coupe
GARNISH: chocolate curls

Pour all ingredients into a shaker
with ice. Shake for at least one to
two minutes until nice and frothy,
then strain into glass. Garnish with
chocolate curls.

. . . .

Grasshopper Kringle
(Kringle Cream Liqueur)

Jeff Wimmer, who recently passed on the reins of The Del-Bar to his daughter Amy (his parents took over this legendary establishment in 1943), says that the Del-Bar has been serving ice cream drinks since at least the 1950s and most likely the 1940s. At that time, he says, other places around the country made creamy drinks with half-and-half or whipped cream.

"Ice cream drinks have just kind of always been part of our menu," says his daughter. "My grandmother used to make them at dinner parties. And she'd even serve us kids Grasshoppers, but I don't think she served us a lot of alcohol in them. I think it was just a dash of flavoring."

By the 1960s and the 1970s, ice cream drinks were so well established that supper clubs, restaurants, and bars throughout the state advertised them as specialty drinks—and several places, especially around Mother's Day, offered free ice cream drinks to women. Also, what's notable is that classified advertisements for bartenders often contained the requirement "must have knowledge of blended and ice cream drinks." By the late 1980s, bar supplies included custard machines that were especially made for ice cream drinks, too.

While the Brandy Alexander and the Grasshopper don't have Wisconsin origins, three ice cream drinks likely do, and they got their start at Bryant's Cocktail Lounge, which is the oldest cocktail lounge in Milwaukee and perhaps the entire state. Before it was a cocktail lounge, Bryant Sharp opened it in 1936 with his wife Edna as a beer hall. But in 1938 he converted it to a swanky cocktail lounge, which it remained, even after a fire in 1971.

According to local bar lore and some written records at Bryant's, Sharp invented the Pink Squirrel, the Blue Tail Fly, and the Banshee.

Like other noted bartenders of his era, Sharp created drink recipes and cordial flavors, which he then sold to liquor companies, who promoted them. Sharp died in 1959, and Bryant's was taken over by Pat Malmberg, a bartender who moved to Milwaukee in 1947. According to an interview with the *Milwaukee Journal* on June 23, 1985, Malberg said Sharp created the Banshee in 1951.

Dye, who took over Bryant's in 2008, says he's not quite sure if these drinks were cream-based or ice cream-based. "We found old records from the 1950s that referenced both types of drinks," Dye says.

Dye says that what he does know from talking to Ron Zeller—from whom Dye bought At Random in 2018—is that the drinks at At Random were first made with cream and then they added ice cream a little bit later on. Zeller, it should be noted, worked for Sharp before going on to open At Random, which is Milwaukee's second oldest cocktail lounge.

While not many bartenders in Milwaukee will quibble about this origin story, some bar historians aren't so certain that Sharp invented the Pink Squirrel, as the earliest print references aren't from Milwaukee. They're from New York City, and they were all about a publicity stunt for the cocktail in early June 1951. Singer Betty Reed made the rounds of New York City bars with an actual pink squirrel, to promote the Pink Squirrel cocktail for liquor company Bols. This story—and variations of it—were published in several New York City publications, and then it hit the Associated Press wire, and it was republished in the *Milwaukee Journal* on June 15, 1951.

There aren't any records that dispute Sharp's story—that he created it and sold it to liquor companies—but officials for the Bols company "could not confirm" any storeis about the drink's origins.

What is known is that the second Wisconsin newspaper reference is from Buck Herzog's April 24, 1952, *Milwaukee Sentinel* column, where he highlights some interesting cocktails local bartenders were suggesting. "Chances are, he'll have some strange sounding new concoctions on tap for you. Among the names that will take on new meaning across the bars are White Cloud, Big Apple, Pink Squirrel, Salty Dog, Gimlet, Screwdriver, and Cucumber." If the Pink Squirrel made its public debut in 1951, Wisconsinites caught on pretty fast to this drinking trend.

A year later, on October 11, 1953, the *Milwaukee Sentinel*'s "Dining for the Discriminating" restaurant reviewer featured the Tam O'Shanter Club on Bluemound Road, mentioning that one of the specialty cocktails in the lounge was called the Pink Squirrel. "It contains equal portions of cream, white crème de cacao and cream de noya, the latter providing the pink color."

PINK SQUIRREL

½ oz. crème de noyaux
½ oz. white crème de cacao
3 scoops vanilla ice cream

GLASS: poco, hurricane, or rocks
GARNISH: homemade whipped cream and drizzle of crème de noyaux

Pour crème de noyaux and crème de cacao into the bottom of a blender. Top with ice cream. Blend until creamy and smooth. Pour into glass, top with homemade whipped cream, then drizzle crème de noyaux on top.

VELVET HAMMER

Amy Wimmer, owner, The Del-Bar, Wisconsin Dells

½ oz. white crème de cacao
½ oz. Cointreau, or other orange liqueur
3 scoops vanilla ice cream

GLASS: poco, hurricane, or rocks
GARNISH: homemade whipped cream

Pour crème de cacao and Cointreau into the bottom of a blender.
Top with ice cream. Blend until creamy and smooth. Pour into glass,
top with homemade whipped cream.

. . . .

BLUE TAIL FLY

½ oz. Blue Curaçao
½ oz. white crème de cacao
3 scoops ice cream

GLASS: poco, hurricane, or rocks
GARNISH: homemade whipped cream and drizzle of Blue Curaçao

Pour Blue Curaçao and crème de cacao into the bottom of a blender.
Top with ice cream. Blend until creamy and smooth. Pour into glass, top
with homemade whipped cream, then drizzle Blue Curaçao on top.

. . . .

BANSHEE

½ oz. crème de banana
½ oz. white crème de cacao
3 scoops vanilla ice cream
1 banana, peeled and cut into chunks

GLASS: poco, hurricane, or rocks
GARNISH: homemade whipped cream and chocolate-dipped banana

Pour crème de banana and crème de cacao into the bottom of a blender. Top with ice cream and banana pieces. Blend until creamy and smooth. Pour into glass, top with homemade whipped cream, then garnish with a chocolate-dipped banana.

....

GOLDEN CADILLAC

½ oz. Galliano
½ oz. white crème de cacao
3 scoops vanilla ice cream

GLASS: poco, hurricane, or rocks
GARNISH: homemade whipped cream and drizzle of Galliano

Pour Galliano and crème de cacao into the bottom of a blender. Top with ice cream. Blend until creamy and smooth. Pour into a glass, top with homemade whipped cream, then drizzle Galliano on top.

....

Throughout the 1950s and 1960s, liquor advertisements in Wisconsin newspapers promoted cordials to make Alexanders, Pink Squirrels, and Grasshoppers at home, and by the 1970s, readymade mixers with booze in them were advertised for sale at liquor stores for Pink Squirrels, Grasshoppers, Alexanders, and more. In fact, at Martinique Supper Club, New Year's Eve in 1960 was celebrated with "all you want to drink" Grasshoppers, Pink Ladies, Banshees, Martinis, Manhattans, Old Fashioneds, scotch, bourbon, Pink Squirrels, and champagne.

What was served in the bar also migrated into the kitchen, as enterprising home cooks began turning drink recipes into pies and other baked goods. Perhaps the two most interesting desserts were a Pink Squirrel fondue and a Brandy Alexander soufflé. By the 1970s, they were seemingly everywhere. Dennis Ghetto, a Milwaukee restaurant critic, noted that ice cream drinks were integral to a group of couples who regularly participated in progressive dinner parties in Oak Creek. These drinks were such a part of their dinners that they regularly razzed one guy, who once forgot to have the necessary ingredients on hand to make them.

Today, on any given night at a supper club or bar, ice cream drinks are blended, whirled, and even whipped up in soft-serve machines. And places that serve ice cream drinks don't ever make just a few ice cream drinks in a night, says Amy Wimmer. They make thousands of them in any given week. Groups will come in and preorder them by the dozen, and sometimes, instead of full-sized drinks, they order mini Grasshoppers and mini Brandy Alexanders, too. "There are nights when we make fifty at a time," she says.

Ice cream drinks, says Scotty McCormick, head bartender of Lola's Restaurant at the Osthoff Resort in Elkhart Lake, are the kind of cocktails that turn heads, and as soon as one person orders one, other people start craving them. If the bar or restaurant doesn't have a good system for executing them quickly, they can become the bane of a bartender's existence, he says. McCormick says that when he worked at the Paddock Club, he convinced the owner to get rid of the blenders because it was so time consuming to go down to the basement, get the ice cream, mix up the drinks in the blender, and bring them upstairs to serve. The owner took his advice, and the blenders were removed, and so ice cream drink lovers were sent next door to the Lake Street Café. "Eventually, I ended up at the Lake Street Café, so I was making ice cream drinks again," McCormick says.

They are such a pain to make that Corinna Todd, who owns the Red Pines Bar & Tavern in Onalaska with her husband, doesn't list ice cream drinks on their menu, even though their bartenders will make them. "The last thing you want to do when you're three-deep at the bar is make an ice cream drink," she says. "Our bartenders have to go into the kitchen to make them."

MUDSLIDE SHAKE

Matt Tunnel, mixologist, Great Lakes Distillery, Milwaukee

1 oz. Roaring Dan's rum, or other rum
1 oz. Good Land Valentine Coffee Liqueur, or other coffee liqueur
½ cup vanilla or chocolate ice cream

GLASS: martini, coupe, Collins, or rocks
GARNISH: drizzle of chocolate sauce

Pour rum and coffee liqueur into a blender, top with ice cream, and blend until smooth. Drizzle chocolate sauce into glass and pour in boozy shake. If you would like, drizzle chocolate sauce in the glass, then pour some of the shake, then drizzle layers of chocolate sauce between additional layers of shake.

Cookies & Cream Milkshake (Kringle Cream Liqueur)

Mudslide Shake at Great Lakes Distillery
(Great Lakes Distillery)

NUTORIOUS PBC

Don's Diner, Milwaukee

1 oz. Skrewball peanut butter whiskey, or other whiskey
⅓ oz. chocolate syrup
4 scoops vanilla ice cream

GLASS: shake
GARNISH: crumbled Reese's Peanut Butter Cups, whipped cream,
more Reese's Peanut Butter Cups

Place all ingredients into a blender and blend until smooth. To serve, pour half of the mixture into the bottom of the shake glass, then half of the crumbled Reese's Peanut Butter Cups, then the rest of the shake. Top with whipped cream and the remaining Reese's Peanut Butter Cups.

. . . .

COOKIES & CREAM MILKSHAKE

Kringle Cream mixologists

2 oz. Kringle Cream liqueur, or other cream liqueur
1 oz. vanilla vodka
2 scoops vanilla or coffee ice cream
4 chocolate sandwich cookies

GLASS: shake or Collins
GARNISH: whipped cream, chocolate syrup, and chocolate sandwich cookies

Place all ingredients into a blender and blend until smooth. Pour into glass. Top with whipped cream, drizzle with chocolate syrup, and finish with chocolate sandwich cookies.

. . . .

SPANISH DELIGHT

Don's Diner, Milwaukee

1 oz. Don Q rum, or other rum
⅓ oz. State Line coffee liqueur, or other coffee liqueur
½ oz. dulce de leche syrup
½ oz. whole milk
3 scoops vanilla ice cream

GLASS: shake
GARNISH: churro, whipped cream, and dulce de leche syrup

Place all ingredients into a blender and blend until smooth. Pour into a shake glass. Put churro on top, then top with whipped cream and lavishly pour dulce de leche syrup on top of that.

You can buy dulce de leche syrup (especially online), but the easiest way to make it is to take a can of sweetened condensed milk, remove the label and all the glue, then submerge the can in a pot of water, with at least two inches of water over the top of the can. Simmer for two to three hours, never letting the water boil off so the can is exposed (you will likely need to add more hot water as you cook it). Then let it cool completely, remove the lid, and scoop out the dulce de leche. To make it of drizzling consistency, you will need to warm it up again.

. . . .

YABBA DABBA DO IT

Don's Diner, Milwaukee

1 oz. Korbel brandy, or other brandy
⅓ oz. Cartron Marasquin liqueur, or other cherry liqueur
2 tbsp. crushed Fruity Pebbles cereal, or other fruit-flavored cereal
4 scoops vanilla ice cream

GLASS: shake
GARNISH: 2 cake balls, whipped cream, and crushed Fruity Pebbles cereal

Place all ingredients into a blender and blend until smooth. Pour into a shake glass. Top with cake balls, then top with whipped cream and more crushed Fruity Pebbles cereal.

Cartron Marasquin is a liqueur made from small, bitter cherries grown in Croatia. It is a very balanced, slightly sweet liqueur with a pronounced stone cherry flavor. If you can't find it, you can substitute with another cherry liqueur. Cake balls are basically mini cakes cooked into ball shapes. You can buy them at bakeries and at some coffee chains, but you can also make them at home with cake pop kits.

. . . .

Over the years, "diet" versions of the cocktails have come out, with fat-free frozen yogurt and low-fat or fat-free nondairy topping subbing for ice cream. Some bartenders and home enthusiasts don't drink dairy, so they've adapted classic ice cream cocktails by using soy, coconut, and almond-milk ice creams, or they simply use a non-dairy cream with ice. Rachel Werner, a digital media expert, model, and writer based in Madison, still craves ice cream drinks—even though she's adopted a vegan lifestyle. She simply replaces ice cream with nondairy ingredients in her favorite ice cream drinks. "Booze is vegetarian," Werner says. "Toast to a Wisconsin summer well spent, and hopefully a long autumn on the horizon!"

To make a cream version of any of these drinks, skip the ice cream and pour 1 oz. of each liquor the recipes call for and 1 oz. of either heavy cream or half-and-half into a shaker filled with ice. Shake for one to two minutes and then strain into a glass, preferably a coupe or martini glass.

Yabba Dabba Do It at Don's Diner (Stand Eat Drink)

Pu-Erh Grasshopper Milkshake
(Brian West, *Alcoholmanac*)

PU-ERH GRASSHOPPER MILKSHAKE

Kurt Fogle, first published by Brian West in *Alcoholmanac*, 2013

½ cup Pu-Erh-infused milk
1 cup Purple Door mint chip ice cream
1¼ oz. Cocoa-Nib-Infused American Harvest organic spirit or vodka
1 oz. hot fudge

GLASS: Collins
GARNISH: fresh mint leaves and tempered chocolate curl

Place all ingredients into a blender and blend until smooth. Garnish
with fresh mint leaves and tempered chocolate.

Pu-Erh-infused milk can be made by combining ½ oz. Rishi Tea Pu-Erh
Vanilla tea (or other Pu-Erh tea and a vanilla bean) and 2¼ cups Sassy
Cow Creamery whole milk (or other milk). Infuse for three to four days,
minimum twelve hours.

The restaurant method for making cocoa-nib-infused spirit is to add
1¾ oz. roasted Valrhona cocoa nibs (or other cocoa nibs) and 1 cup
American Harvest organic spirit (or other vodka) to an iSi cream
whipper and charge with two rounds of nitrous oxide. Allow to infuse
for three hours. The home method is to combine spirits and cocoa nibs
in a bottle and let it sit for a minimum of two weeks.

....

BRANDY FROST (VEGAN)

Rachel Werner, digital media artist, fitness model, and writer, Madison

1 pint mint chip nondairy frozen dessert, like So Delicious coconut-milk ice cream
1 cup almond or oat milk
4 oz. Kohler Dark Chocolate Brandy, or other brandy
2 oz. Yahara Bay Cocoa Liqueur, or other chocolate liqueur
¼ cup organic cane sugar

Chill four martini glasses for at least thirty minutes. In the meantime, mix together the frozen dessert, milk, and brandy using a blender. Remove martini glasses from the freezer and rim each with a generous amount of cane sugar. Then add a small amount of the cocoa liqueur into the bottom of each glass before filling with brandy "milkshake."

. . . .

AVOCADO LEMONGRASS LAVENDER CIDER ICE CREAM

Scott Phillips, owner, Brasserie V, Madison

ICE CREAM BASE

2 cup heavy cream
1 cup whole milk
1 tsp. salt
1 cup sugar
1 tbsp. vanilla extract
3 egg yolks

Fill large metal mixing bowl with ice and water to chill. Heat cream, milk, and salt to simmer in a thick-bottomed pan. Whisk sugar and vanilla extract into the egg yolks in a separate pan. Remove cream mixture from heat and slowly incorporate the egg yolk mixture, being careful not to curdle the yolks. Strain the custard through a fine mesh strainer into the chilled mixing bowl and refrigerate for at least two hours.

AVOCADO PUREE

1 lime, juiced

4 oz. Lemongrass Lavender Cider by Hidden Cave Cidery, or other hard cider

2 avocados

¼ cup honey

Cayenne pepper to taste

Combine lime juice and cider in a saucepan until reduced by half. In a food processor slowly blend the avocados and cider reduction. Add honey at the end and chill.

To make final ice cream: spin the ice cream base and avocado puree in your ice cream maker according to manufacturer standards, then set aside in freezer for two to three hours. Season with cayenne to taste. Don't have an ice cream maker? Don't worry! Just substitute three cups vanilla ice cream for the base and mix with avocado puree in a blender on medium to high until smooth.

....

CHOCOLATE AND ORANGE MEZCAL MILKSHAKE

Kurt Fogle, first published by Brian West in *Alcoholmanac*, 2013

1 cup Purple Door milk chocolate ice cream, or other ice cram

3½ oz. orange-cinnamon milk

⅓ oz. orange juice concentrate

1 oz. mezcal

GLASS: rocks

GARNISH: chocolate shavings, orange peel, and toasted cinnamon stick

Place all ingredients into a blender and blend until smooth. Garnish with chocolate shavings, an orange peel, and a toasted cinnamon stick.

Orange-cinnamon milk can be made by combining ¼ oz. orange zest, ⅛ oz. toasted cinnamon stick, and 2¼ cups Sassy Cow Creamery whole milk (or other milk).

....

Chocolate and Orange Mezcal Milkshake (Brian West, *Alcoholmanac*)

Door County Cherry and Gin Milkshake (Brian West, *Alcoholmanac*)

DOOR COUNTY CHERRY AND GIN MILKSHAKE

Kurt Fogle, first published by Brian West in *Alcoholmanac*, 2013

1 oz. Door County cherry jam, or other jam

3½ oz. Sassy Cow Creamery whole milk, or other milk

1 oz. sugar cookie

1 cup Purple Door vanilla bean ice cream, or other ice cream

1¼ oz. Great Northern Distilling Herbalist gin, or other gin

GLASS: Collins

GARNISH: sugar cookie crumbles and fresh cherry

Place all ingredients into a blender and blend until smooth. Garnish with sugar cookie crumbles and a fresh cherry.

. . . .

№ 5

HOT TODDIES, BUTTERED RUM, AND COFFEE COCKTAILS

WARM DRINKS TO WARD OFF WISCONSIN WINTERS

WHILE OUR DAIRY COWS ARE ACTUALLY HAP-PIEST WHEN OUR TEMPERATURES DROP TO BETWEEN 40 AND 50 DEGREES, THE REST OF US DO NOT ALWAYS APPRECIATE THE CHILL. AND EVEN IF WE'RE WINTER SPORTS AFICIONADOS WHO SKI, SKATE, SNOWMOBILE, OR DOGSLED, WE USUALLY NEED TO WARM UP IF WE'VE BEEN OUTSIDE (EVEN IF IT'S JUST TO CONVINCE OUR ERRANT TERRIER THAT SHE REALLY DOES NEED TO POTTY DURING A SNOWSTORM).

Which is why it's no surprise that when the nights grow longer and we've taken our parkas and long underwear out of storage, we hearty Wisconsinites switch out our brandy slushes for brandy toddies.

Hot toddies, hot buttered rum, and hot coffee drinks all rise in popularity in the fall and winter seasons, and sometimes we even drink them into spring and summer when the forecast is gray and cold, and the actual season doesn't match the dates on the calendar.

Toddy-ing Along

While the word "toddy" likely comes from either an Allan Ramsay poem, published in 1781 about the Todian Spring in Scotland, or an Indian beverage made from palm tree sap, the drink definitely has been around for centuries, served in pubs, saloons, and taverns wherever blustery climes moved in or whenever medicinally necessary.

Unlike many cocktails, which involve exact measurements, hot toddies have not traditionally called for them. They consist of booze (whiskey, brandy, rum, etc.), a hot beverage (cider, water, tea), a sweetener (sugar, honey, molasses, etc.), and citrus and/or spices (lemon or lime, cloves, cinnamon, etc.).

Any booze will do for the spirit, and since they likely originated in Scotland or England, the choice of spirit was usually Scotch or whiskey. Here in Wisconsin, though, a hot toddy is as likely to be made with brandy as it is with any type of whiskey (or "whisky," depending on its origin). In fact, one of my favorite old newspaper stories was about a dramatic rescue of a teenaged girl who fell into Green Bay and survived in its rough, cold waters. Her rescuers took her to the nearest house, where she was covered with blankets and revived with brandy. You can also use rum or liqueurs . . . really, any booze will do.

The liquid can be cider, tea, water—or even wine, or a juice other than apple. The sweetener is often sugar or honey, but today it can be molasses, maple syrup, sorghum, stevia, or even fruit juice concentrates. The spices are typically cloves, cinnamon, nutmeg, or allspice; the citrus, while usually lemon, can also be lime or grapefruit or orange, and while cranberry isn't a citrus fruit, it is tangy, and it, too, can be used.

Irish Coffee Culture

While the toddy has been around for centuries, the Irish coffee hasn't reached its centennial yet. Joe Sheridan, the enterprising bartender at the Foynes (now Shannon) International Airport, is credited with its creation. The story goes that a plane, which had been headed to the United States in 1943, had to turn around because of inclement weather, and Sheridan was asked to create a warming drink for the disembarking passengers. Sheridan combined sugar, Irish whiskey, and hot coffee, topping it with cream, and it was a hit. Some accounts say he invented it; others say it was invented elsewhere and that Sheridan simply served it to passengers.

Two journalists are credited with bringing the recipe back to the United States and introducing it to Americans. While Stanley Delaplane of the *San Francisco Chronicle* is believed to have introduced the idea in 1951 to the owner of San Francisco's Buena Vista Café, Jack Koeppler, who later then brought Sheridan over to his café to make the cocktail, Delaplane isn't the first journalist to write about the coffee.

That first mention belongs to the food critic of the *New York Herald Sun*, Clementine Paddleford. Paddleford, who was a licensed pilot and adventurer, experienced the coffee at the airport, and she was so enchanted that she tracked down the recipe from Pan American World Airways ground hostess Maureen Grogan and wrote a story about it. She then published her account, and the recipe, on St. Patrick's Day in 1948. Although she got the recipe first, the drink didn't take off in New York City—it took off in San Francisco.

And it actually came to Wisconsin by way of California. Jim Koconis, the *Milwaukee Sentinel*'s "Night Life Chatter" columnist, wrote about a new drink on December 7, 1957. He reported that "a drink called 'Irish Coffee' is being featured at Ray Jackson's Supper Club. It was introduced to Ray by the Los Angeles Rams who happened to be in town. Contents: Irish whisky, hot coffee, whipped cream." A year later, the Kaiser Knickerbocker hotel and café advertised "Another

First in Milwaukee . . . Irish Coffee," and by 1959 it was being served all over both the city and the state on St. Patrick's Day.

But perhaps my favorite historic reference from the early days of Irish coffee is that a June 14, 1959, *Milwaukee Sentinel* article about Mrs. Helen Raab—who was turning over her Dawn Manor property, house, and art collection to the Wisconsin State Historical Society—had a whole section devoted to her friend, a Miss Grace Niles. It seems Niles would pick up her Sunday *Sentinel* at the Lake Delton drugstore and "bring one along for Mrs. Raab. Her 'pay' for this service is a cup of Irish coffee."

The drink trended in popularity throughout winter months in the 1960s and 1970s, and it became the basis for whipped cream pies, parfaits, and even an Irish coffee gelatin mold recipe, which ran in the *Milwaukee Sentinel* in 1963 . . . that particular recipe is about as unappetizing as you might imagine it to be.

Other spirits began being added to coffee as early as 1960—everything from kirsch to crème de menthe—and by the late 1970s and early 1980s these fortified coffees had become a brunch staple. Things got even fancier when The Coffee Trader opened in the 1970s: besides espresso and fancy nonalcoholic coffees, its signature drink was the Coffee Trader, which was made with espresso, cocoa, whipped cream, and Amaretto.

But as different liquors and liqueurs began to be added to coffee, the original Irish coffee recipe was diluted. By the 1980s, restaurants and bars were advertising both Irish coffee and Irish crème, and some liquor stores were advertising Irish cream liqueurs that came with "Irish coffee mugs."

Paul Ward, manager of Ashling on the Lough in Kenosha, has

strong feelings on the subject of Irish coffee, especially when it's listed on a restaurant or bar menu. "A lot of what is sold as Irish coffee is not real Irish coffee," says Ward. "I'm not only Irish, but I'm a bartender—so when I go to a place that serves Irish coffee, nine times out of ten, it's not an Irish coffee. Irish coffee will never be made with Bailey's or a bit of crème de menthe on the top. As with the culture of Ireland, it's all about simplicity."

A true Irish coffee has just a hint of sweetness, Ward says. A real Irish coffee contains Irish whiskey, just a touch of sugar, really good coffee, and real, unadulterated whipped cream. "It should never be stuff out of the can," Ward chides. The resulting cocktail should never be cloying, and the cream itself should never, ever be sweetened.

It also shouldn't be too boozy, and it should be made with quality coffee. Ward's personal preference is Valentine Coffee, but any really good coffee will do.

The other big quibble Ward has is that most Irish coffees are not served properly. By the time they reach the guest, they're lukewarm. They should be hot, and the best way to ensure this is to warm the mug with boiling water before making the cocktail.

Ward says he has nothing against other coffee cocktails, even those made with Irish cream liqueurs. "A Bailey's and coffee is great, but it's not an Irish coffee," Ward says.

Now, most Wisconsinites aren't this uptight about Irish coffee, and most aren't such purists. In fact, plenty of bartenders and customers prefer to have a sweeter and sometimes boozier concoction.

Mark Dougherty, who owns Mark's East Side in Appleton, says that part of the fun in creating an Irish coffee is to put your own unique spin on it. "What we do is a little bit different," Dougherty

Irish Coffee at Ashling on the Lough (Harp & Eagle LTD)

says. "It's not just whiskey. We add a little bit of coffee liqueur, Kahlua, to it, then we top it with crème de menthe. It all kind of mixes happily together. The little bit of coffee flavor warms the drink up a bit, otherwise it's just booze and coffee."

Dougherty says that one other important difference is in the kind of sugar to use. He uses Sugar in the Raw. "You could use any sugar, but we like using natural sugar," Dougherty says.

Corinna Todd, who owns the Red Pines Bar & Grill in Onalaska, says that sweet coffee drinks are like dessert in winter. "In winter, people really want to splurge on something, to have a dessert drink that's hot," Todd says. "And it's definitely a dessert."

Brian West, who owns Crucible Beverage Company and has

published *Alcoholmanac* magazine in Milwaukee, says that one trend of coffee cocktails is to use cold brew or cold coffee in recipes instead of just making hot coffee cocktails, especially when they're made with locally roasted coffees. "We have a stronger coffee culture than even Chicago, and we're Milwaukee and Madison," says West. "We're tiny [compared to Chicago], and we have these fantastic roasters, and they're all so very different from each other. I can taste a coffee blind, and I can tell you the name of the roaster—they're that distinct from each other. And they make great coffee cocktails."

IRISH COFFEE

Paul Ward, general manager, Ashling on the Lough, Kenosha

1½ oz. Irish whiskey
1 flat tsp. brown sugar
3 to 4 oz. black coffee
real whipped cream, unsweetened

GLASS: eight-ounce Irish coffee mug

Fill an Irish coffee mug with boiling water. Discard the water and pour sugar and whiskey into the bottom of the warmed mug. Top with hot coffee, then stir briskly, churning the spoon from the bottom of the cup so the whiskey and sugar mix into the coffee. Then, gently spoon on whipped cream and sip through a straw. "The idea is that you are supposed to drink the beverage through the cream, and you're not supposed to stir it up," Ward says.

The whipped cream should be pure, unadulterated, real cream. Don't buy fake stuff, Ward says, and don't sweeten the whipped cream at all. To make sure you're buying real whipping cream, read the ingredients listed on the carton. It should list just one, single ingredient: cream. Many unsweetened whipping creams have thickening additives like carrageenan and guar gum. If you are using pure heavy cream, those won't be listed. Sassy Cow Creamery, a Wisconsin-based dairy, makes a heavy cream that is just pure cream, and it's found in many grocery stores throughout the state.

....

WISCONSIN STYLE IRISH COFFEE

Mark Dougherty, owner, Mark's East Side, Appleton

1 tsp. Sugar in the Raw, or other natural sugar
1 oz. Jameson Irish whiskey, or other whiskey
¼ oz. Kahlua, or other coffee liqueur
3 to 4 oz. hot coffee

GLASS: Irish coffee mug
GARNISH: whipped cream and drizzle of crème de menthe

Fill a mug with boiling water. Discard water. Add sugar, whiskey, and Kahlua and stir until sugar is almost dissolved. Add coffee, top with whipped cream, and drizzle crème de menthe on top.

....

CARAMEL IRISH COFFEE

Corinna Todd, owner, Red Pines Bar & Grill, Onalaska

1½ oz. Tulamore Dew Irish whiskey, or other whiskey
¾ oz. Irish crème liqueur
¾ oz. butterscotch schnapps
3 to 4 oz. hot coffee

GLASS: Irish coffee mug
GARNISH: whipped cream with a drizzle of caramel and/or chocolate sauce

Fill a mug with boiling water. Discard water. Add all spirits, top with hot coffee and whipped cream, and garnish with a drizzle of caramel and/or chocolate sauce.

....

Salted Caramel Wakeup (Kringle Cream Liqueur)

Coffee Julep (Brian West, *Alcoholmanac*)

SALTED CARAMEL WAKEUP

Kringle Cream mixologists

8 oz. hot coffee
2 oz. Kringle Cream Liqueur
1 oz. coffee liqueur
1 tbsp. caramel syrup
¼ tsp. salt

GLASS: Irish coffee mug
GARNISH: whipped cream and caramel syrup

Fill a mug with boiling water. Discard water. Pour coffee into warmed mug. Add Kringle Cream liqueur, coffee liqueur, caramel syrup, and salt. Stir, then top with whipped cream and caramel syrup.

COFFEE JULEP

Brian West with several Milwaukee bartenders in a workshop, first published in *Alcoholmanac*, 2018

5 to 6 fresh large mint leaves
1 oz. Hawthorne El Salvador coffee simple syrup, or other coffee
2 oz. of Suntory Toki Japanese whiskey, or other whiskey

GLASS: rocks or Collins
GARNISH: 3 coffee beans

Directly in your serving glass, muddle mint very gently with coffee simple syrup (over-muddling will cause the mint to release bitter flavors and overwhelm some of its more delicate nuances, critical to a well-balanced julep). Fill the glass half full with small ice cubes (or crushed ice). Add Suntory Toki and give it a few quick stirs. Top with more crushed ice and more fresh mint, spanked to release aromatics. Top with 3 coffee beans.

To make the Hawthorne El Salvador coffee simple syrup combine two parts sugar to one part hot, freshly brewed coffee (i.e., two cups sugar to one cup coffee). Stir (or place in heat-resistant sealable container and shake) until completely dissolved. You may need to combine in a saucepan and heat until sugar is dissolved. Store in a heat-resistant container and refrigerate between uses.

....

Buttering Up to Buttered Rum

Hot buttered rum is basically a hot toddy made of rum with a pat of butter melted in for texture and comfort. It was definitely a colonial-era drink, as the original American colonies imported rum from the Caribbean, and according to an article published in the Milwaukee Sentinel in 1957, it was originally made by sticking a hot poker in a mug or tankard containing the mixture. "Today pokers are not as common as they once were. However, a delicious hot buttered rum can be prepared more safely without the aid of a glowing poker."

Hot buttered rum experienced a revival, of sorts, in the late 1930s and early 1940s, after Kenneth Roberts published his historical novel *Northwest Passage*, which included a reference to the cocktail. His character, Cap Huff, demonstrates how to properly make the drink by combining two cups of maple sugar into an inch of hot water, then drowning that with two quarts of rum, a lump of butter "the size of his fist," and a handful of powdered cinnamon. "This here," he said, "aint the proper way to make it. I put hot water in this here, but what you ought to have is hot cider. You take three or four drinks of this, made the right way, and you don't worry about what kind of food you're eating, or about anything else, either. You can't even remember what you et five minutes after you et it."

MRS. KARL RATZCH'S HOT BUTTERED RUM

from the *Milwaukee Journal,* 1948

1 tsp. brown sugar
1 oz. light rum
½ oz. dark Jamaica rum
twisted lemon rind
1 pat of butter

GLASS: mug
GARNISH: lemon rind, grated cinnamon or nutmeg, and cinnamon stick

In an eight-ounce mug, pour brown sugar, rums, and add lemon rind. Fill the mug with boiling water. Add pat of butter, sprinkle with grated cinnamon or nutmeg. Stick cinnamon is preferred.

. . . .

Dorothy Parnell, the *Milwaukee Sentinel* women's editor, instructed her readers in 1951 thus: "To make a hot buttered rum, you need a copper or pewter pitcher to make the drink. Bring the cider to a boil, filling the room with a delicate fragrance. Into a copper mug or pewter mug, decant two ounces of rum and one ounce of brandy. Drop in a clove, a modest strip of lemon peel and a stick of cinnamon. Fill the mug nearly full with the boiling cider, swish it around with a spoon to assure proper blending, top with a pat of butter . . . and ceremoniously serve to eager guests. You can omit the rum and brandy and still have a pleasant drink for teetotalers."

Now, what you'll notice in Parnell's recipe is that it is really a hot buttered rum and brandy recipe, not just rum, which is how we like our Tom and Jerrys, too. What's also interesting is that in an article published in the *Milwaukee Journal* in 1969 on the many drinks that Wisconsin skiers enjoy after a run down the slopes, one skier swore that hot buttered brandy was better than hot buttered rum, and that he basically took a hot buttered rum recipe and just substituted brandy for the rum. Now, this same article also recommended "a nutritious blend for the whole family is a large can (46 ounces) of vegetable juice, heated with a tablespoon of lemon juice and one-half teaspoon of dried dill leaves." (Personally, hot V8 juice just gives me the heeby jeebies, but then again this is the same era that gave us the glorious Irish coffee gelatin molds, too.)

In Wisconsin, hot buttered rum became a fashionable après-ski sipper, and almost any article about winter sports mentioned how good it tasted after being outside in our winter wonderland. My favorite such mention was by Jay Scriba, who penned this in his Wisconsin Notes, published in the *Milwaukee Journal* on February 11, 1979: "Matronly woman on skis at top of Mt. La Crosse: 'It seems like an awful lot to go through for hot buttered rum.' From Chuck Masters, in the *Monroe County Democrat*, Sparta."

But whether the drink was made with cider or water, or served after skiing or snowmobiling, the key was that pat of butter. And that's what some more modern drinkers quibble with—that a pat of butter, by itself, might just leave an oily residue rather than adding a silky texture. So what some modern mixologists do is mix equal parts butter and ice cream, along with sugar and spices, then freeze the whole thing together. And that sounds just a bit like another hot Wisconsin beverage, the Tom and Jerry.

A QUICK AND HOT BUTTERED RUM

1 tbsp. unsalted butter, preferably heavier in milkfat

1 tbsp. maple syrup or brown sugar

¼ tsp. cinnamon

⅛ tsp. nutmeg

⅛ tsp. ground cloves

⅛ tsp. allspice

¼ tsp. vanilla extract

1 dash Angostura bitters, or other bitters

1½ to 2 oz. rum like Roaring Dan's rum (which has maple syrup), or other rum

4 to 5 oz. hot water

GLASS: mug or glass mug
GARNISH: cinnamon stick

Soften butter in microwave for ten to fifteen seconds. Whisk butter with maple syrup, spices, vanilla extract, and bitters. Set aside. Fill a mug with boiling water. Discard water. Pour rum into the bottom of the mug, top with hot water, add butter mixture. Whisk briskly, add cinnamon stick, and enjoy.

Instead of hot water, you can also substitute hot cider or tea. Chamomile tea, brewed before pouring over the rum and butter mixture, works really well. If you wish to make this creamier, add 1 tbsp. vanilla or cinnamon ice cream to the butter mixture, then chill before using.

Mulling Over Mulled Wine

Mulled wine is the great-granddaddy of all hot beverages. Its history is, well, not quite as old as wine, but historical records show that both the ancient Greeks and the ancient Romans drank mulled wine. It was also quite popular during the Middle Ages, but what we think of as mulled wine comes mainly from the Victorian era, as it was often served during the holidays and winter months.

Here in Wisconsin it was enjoyed before we were actually a state, and it has been enjoyed pretty much ever since. One of my favorite articles about mulled wine comes from a *Milwaukee Journal* article about entertaining for a "Hallow E'en Party (Ways in Which Simple Refresh-ments Should Be Served)" that dates back to October 22, 1894. Dug-out pumpkins were recommended, as were doughnuts. "It is very nice to have mulled wine to serve with the doughnuts." This same article also recommended mulled "butter milk." Fortunately, mulled buttermilk never seemed to catch on.

Mulled wine was served during Prohibition—and mentioned in newspaper articles in passing, as if it were completely acceptable and legal. It also is part of many of our residents' ethnic heritage, being called Swedish glögg, German glühwein, and English mulled wine. It simply never went out of style, and today many of our wineries make some spiced red wine blends to make it even easier to prepare—just heat and serve.

You can also make mulled cider by using hard cider or regular cider, then adding a spirit or two of your choice. Brian Sammons, founder of Twisted Path Distillery in Milwaukee, serves a version of this when Bayview, his neighborhood in Milwaukee, does nighttime trick or treating. Trick or treating is a big event in this part of the city, and neighbors throw bonfires in their front yards while others offer treats to adults who are taking their kids around. Sammons heats up apple cider, then throws in a shot of his chai liqueur. "The best gar-nish for this is Halloween candy," Sammons says.

MULLED WINE

750 ml bottle of red wine

¼ cup brandy

¼ cup sugar

1 orange, cut into slices

4 cinnamon sticks

½ tsp. whole cloves

2 star anise

GLASS: mug

GARNISH: cinnamon stick and orange wheel

Bring all ingredients to a simmer over low heat for about twenty minutes. Remove from heat, strain, and serve.

. . . .

CHAI SPICED CIDER

Brian Sammons, owner, Twisted Path Distillery, Milwaukee

1½ oz. chai liqueur

5 oz. apple cider

GLASS: mug or rocks

GARNISH: Halloween candy

Heat up apple cider. Fill a mug with boiling water. Discard water. Pour in chai liqueur, add apple cider, stir once or twice with a spoon, then garnish with Halloween candy.

For a chilled alternative, place ingredients in a cocktail shaker filled with ice. Shake for sixty seconds, then strain into a rocks glass filled with ice.

Chai Spiced Cider at Twisted Path Distillery
(Twisted Path Distillery)

. . . .

№ 6

BRANDY SLUSHES, CHERRY BOUNCE, AND OTHER WISCONSIN DRINKING HABITS

WE DRINK A LOT OF OTHER THINGS IN WISCONSIN THAT AREN'T NECESSARILY STATE-SPECIFIC, BUT THESE COCKTAILS ARE SO POPULAR THEY DESERVE THEIR OWN MENTION.

While many of these—sweet martinis, whiskey sours, and beers served with shots—originated elsewhere in the country and are popular or used to be popular in other states, these cocktails and habits remain popular here. They deserve their own chapter simply because a lot of people associate them with Wisconsin drinking preferences, and in many cases they've taken on a life of their own here in Wisconsin.

Except for a few of these traditions, most of the things we drink trend sweet: sometimes syrupy sweet, sometimes just delicately sweet, but definitely sweet. "I've actually heard people in the booze industry referring to Wisconsin as having a 'diabetic palate,'" says Brian Sammons, founder and owner of Twisted Path Distillery in Milwaukee. "That's absolutely a thing, especially when distributors from out of state talk to their reps about making drinks in Wisconsin."

While some of these traditions are more bar- and tavern-centric— I'm talking about you, sweet martinis—other traditions are carried out at home.

Perhaps the two biggest of these home-based drinking traditions are brandy slushes and cherry bounce.

Slush Puppies

Slushes, or slushies, as they are sometimes called, are a more recent Wisconsin drinking phenomenon, as they date back to about the 1970s or 1980s.

Slushes are basically summer party cocktails. Mostly, they're frozen or semifrozen drinks made with brandy, but they can be made with vodka, bourbon, or even wine. They typically involve frozen lemonade and/or frozen orange juice concentrate, sometimes tea bags, and basically you mix everything together, including the booze, and then freeze it. But because you add the booze, they never quite freeze all the way through, and they look like the slush on the sidewalk you get when you throw salt out. They're finished off in very Wisconsin fashion: topped with sweet or sour soda.

Julie Phillips, mixologist for the Rittenhouse Inn in Bayfield, makes slushes all the time—just not for her customers at the bed-and-breakfast bar or restaurant. Instead, they're requested by her family, and she makes them not only for summer parties. She even makes them for holiday parties. "There are a billion recipes for slushes—just go on allrecipes.com," Phillips says. "My family loves slushes."

For her family, she uses water, not tea, and she uses a combination of concentrated limeade, lemonade, and orange juice with brandy. "There are other recipes that use apricot brandy or Amaretto or Southern Comfort," Phillips says.

Slushes were pretty commonly requested in Wisconsin newspaper food sections throughout the summer months during the 1980s. But the best historic story is from 1994, when a hippo escaped a game farm in Marquette County, then bathed in the Mecan River before being shot. An enterprising bar owner in Neshkora named a drink after it, which she called the "Hippo Slush." Missy Heller described her creation: "It has apricot brandy on the bottom that looks kind of like river mud. I put green vodka on the top that looks like green water. Everybody loves it." Heller served her cocktail in quart jars filled to the brim, and she charged folks four dollars per quart.

Phillips says that the best part of making a slush is that you don't have to follow an exact recipe—you just mix whatever juices and juice concentrates with whatever liquor or liqueurs you wish. The main thing is that you want to kind of "mix things up" as it freezes. "Otherwise," she says, "you get a liquid center."

BRANDY SLUSH

Matt Tunnel, mixologist, Great Lakes Distillery, Milwaukee

2 cups Brightonwoods apple brandy, or other apple brandy
½ cup Good Land orange liqueur, or other orange liqueur
12 oz. lemonade concentrate, thawed
12 oz. orange juice concentrate, thawed
6 green tea bags
7 cups water
Sprite, or other white soda

GLASS: pint, rocks, poco

Brew the green tea in two cups of water, according to tea instructions. Stir the green tea, brandy, liqueur, lemonade concentrate, orange juice concentrate, and remaining five cups of water until well mixed. Pour into a container, then freeze overnight. To serve, scoop one or two scoops of slush mixture into a glass, then top with white soda.

BRANDY SMASH SLUSH

Katie Wysocki, general manager, Devon Seafood + Steak, Glendale

5 cups freshly made lemonade
3½ cups water
2 cups freshly steeped peach tea, cooled slightly
2 cups peach schnapps
1 cup Wollersheim brandy, or other brandy
12 oz. orange juice concentrate, thawed
1 cup sugar
Sprite to serve

GLASS: rocks or even red Solo cup
GARNISH: fresh peaches, if desired, but totally unnecessary

Whisk all ingredients together, then freeze for at least four hours. To serve, scoop out one large scoop of slush into a glass, top with about 1 oz. Sprite, stir or smash if desired. Enjoy.

....

Cherry Bounce and Apple Pie

The cherry bounce is another one of those seasonal drinks in Wisconsin. But it's made in summer, after picking or buying Door County cherries, which are then mixed with sugar and booze, usually brandy or whiskey, and then it's aged until the holidays hit.

Though this sounds like something we thought up in Wisconsin, the cherry bounce is actually an older cordial—the combination of booze and sugar with a few spices, if you like. It dates back to the late eighteenth century, at least, and it's actually a beverage a guy named George Washington adored. In fact, our very first president liked it so much he poured some in a canteen for his 1784 trip across the Allegheny Mountains. Mount Vernon, his estate, notes this is one of the few recipes they know for certain that he enjoyed, and it's one of the few recipes they actually still have around today.

In Wisconsin, the earliest mentions of cherry bounce are in newspaper advertisements, and they predate our admission to the union as the thirtieth state in 1848. In Milwaukee, in 1847, Ludington & Co. advertised in the *Milwaukee Sentinel & Gazette* that "Raspberry brandy, cherry bounce and peppermint cordial" were for sale. Some folks sold it by the barrel, while others sold it by the bottle. Some places even sold both cherry bounce and raspberry bounce.

In 1894, J. Harvey Meyers, a real estate broker who lived in the suburbs north of Milwaukee, had a cherry orchard on his property. While he was in Milwaukee on business, his wife reported that two men invaded their orchard and absconded with pails of cherries. "Mrs. Meyers saw them. Visions of pickled cherries and preserved cherries, and cherry pie, and it may be cherry bounce began to vanish and give blank despair."

The *Milwaukee Journal*, in 1927, described the historic beverage as "a spirituous liquor with twice the strength of ordinary wine." But perhaps the most interesting historic story about cherry bounce was published in the *Milwaukee Sentinel* on July 21, 1918. The story was about Ephraim Brown Norten, who was celebrating his ninety-second birthday, as he was one of the original pioneers who settled in Mayville, Dodge County. In the article, Norten described life on his farm, including parties. "The drinks for our parties were mostly home made such as currant wine, cherry bounce and raspberry cordial."

While we definitely drank it before we were a state, we kept drinking it during Prohibition. Another article by the *Milwaukee Sentinel*, in 1925, described how 90 percent of our state was violating the law, including "the farmer who squeezes the juice from his apples into cider, Aunt Susie who makes cherry bounce, the neighbor who makes elderberry wine." But in respect for the law, *The Settlement Cookbook*, originally written in 1901 in Milwaukee, omitted all its recipes for booze during Prohibition, but then later added an insert of boozy recipes, including cherry bounce, when repeal happened.

Today, cherry bounce continues as a Wisconsin tradition. A lot of folks make it with brandy, but some prefer whiskey, preferably Canadian rye, and some make it with vodka or bourbon. But it's always made with Door County cherries, and the folks at the Old Fashioned tavern and restaurant in Madison pick some one thousand pounds of cherries, then pack them into brandy, bourbon, and vodka, and about five months later, give or take a few days, they host a cherry bounce party in early December. The party usually features live music, appetizers, and plenty of bounce to go around. They typically serve it . . . until it's gone, and then they don't make any more until the next summer.

Cherry bounce is drunk, straight, and the cherries that are used to make it can then garnish cocktails or be used in desserts—in pies, on ice cream, or just eaten out of the jar.

Now, related to cherry bounce is a concoction called "apple pie." "It's a crazy Wisconsin thing," says Corinna Todd, who co-owns the Red Pines Bar & Grill in Onalaska. Todd learned about it from her bartending staff, as she lived all over the country and all over the world before she and her husband settled in Wisconsin for good.

What it is, she says, is a kind of "apple moonshine." Unlike cherry bounce, which is made in the summer and then drunk over the winter holidays, apple pie is made in the fall and drunk immediately. It's basically (depending on the recipe you use) a mix of Everclear or vodka, fresh apple juice, spices, sugar, and sometimes rum.

It's such a Wisconsin drink that it's even bottled by some Wisconsin distilleries.

BASIC CHERRY BOUNCE

4 cups cherries, with or without pits
750 ml brandy, or other spirit of choice
3 to 4 cups of sugar

Poke each cherry with a fork or knife so that booze can saturate cherries (if you're using pitted cherries, you can skip this step). Set aside. Pour the sugar and the booze into a very large jar you can shake, and shake until mostly dissolved. Add the cherries. If they don't all fit into the same jar, divide between two or more jars. Cover the jars with lids. Let sit for a week in a sunny spot, shaking them occasionally. Then store inside a cupboard or dark space like a pantry for a month or more. When you're ready to drink, strain the juice, and set the cherries aside to use in cocktails or desserts.

Some folks prefer keeping the pits in the cherries so they retain their shape and don't get mushy. Other folks don't care if the cherries get a little lopsided from sitting in the booze and sugar for a month or two. Other people prefer adding cinnamon, cloves, and/or nutmeg to the mixture, but that is up to your own personal preference.

Schnapps and Such

Flavored brandies and schnapps hail back to before Wisconsin was a state, but the first schnapps bear little resemblance to the fruity and minty liqueurs that most of us would recognize as schnapps. In the mid-nineteenth century, ads for Udolpho Wolfe's Aromatic Schiedam Schnapps were common. This schnapps, explains Guy Rehorst, owner and founder of Great Lakes Distillery in Milwaukee, isn't like the schnapps you'll find at a corner bar today in Wisconsin. "Traditionally, German schnapps is not a sweet thing," Rehorst explains.

They're brandies made from different fruits, and they're very dry, Rehorst says, adding that his lineup of fruit brandies are modeled after these traditional German spirits.

In any case, they continued to be consumed in Wisconsin, and by the twentieth century they were so common that a contingent of Wisconsin soldiers, stationed at Camp Wilson in San Antonio, Texas, in 1916, had named its mascot, a little fox terrier, "Schnapps." Schnapps the terrier had been missing for a week, but when a Wisconsin private found him "the cloud of doom that was cast over the battery camp lifted."

But schnapps as we know it, particularly the minty kind, took off after Prohibition, and in Wisconsin it never went away.

The story starts with Ed Phillips emigrating from Minsk, Russia, to Manitowoc. In 1912, at the urging of his son Jay (who was a newspaper boy), he started a wholesale distribution company, selling candy, magazines, and newspapers. Jay, who of course joined his father's company, noticed that after Prohibition many folks would add peppermints to their unaged whiskey. The Phillips company became national liquor distributors, and they started making their own schnapps. Though Phillips Schnapps eventually moved its headquarters to Minneapolis, it still distributes spirits and liqueurs, including that minty kind.

Rehorst says he has another suggestion for why schnapps have always been popular in Wisconsin—we are a more frugal state. "Most really sweet spirits tend to be less expensive than other, less-sweet spirits," Rehorst says. "It's just a theory, though."

Schnapps remains popular in Wisconsin, and plenty of national and local distilleries make sweet liqueurs. Great Lakes makes Good Land cranberry, orange, Door County cherry, and Valentine coffee liqueurs. Twisted Path makes a chai liqueur.

Wisconsinites don't just like sweet liqueurs—they adore sweet, creamy liqueurs. Everything from Bailey's to Rumchata sells well in Wisconsin, particularly around the winter holidays. We like it so much that in 2019, Wisconsin was one of only six states in which Bacardi debuted its limited-release Coquito bottled rum cocktail.

"There's a really strong affinity for cream-based spirits in the Midwest," says Ned Duggan, senior vice president of marketing for Bacardi rum.

The affinity is so strong that Death's Door made a Kringle Cream liqueur, named for the famed buttery Danish pastries in Racine. Margaret Ebeling believed so strongly in Kringle Cream that when Death's Door went bankrupt and she lost her job, she took the liqueur with her. She formed her own liqueur company to save it. "Anyone who knows what a kringle pastry is understands it," Ebeling says.

Ebeling says that the growing popularity of kringle pastries— Trader Joe's sells them around the country—has helped her small spirits company. "But I still need to explain what Kringle Cream is, the further I get from the epicenter of kringle, which is Racine," she says. "Some people think it has to do with Christmas, which it's not."

THE RASPBERRY RUSSIAN

Scotty McCormick, head bartender, Lola's Restaurant,
The Osthoff Resort, Elkhart Lake

1½ oz. Stolichnaya vodka, or other vodka
½ oz. Chambord raspberry liqueur, or other liqueur

GLASS: martini or coupe
GARNISH: fresh or frozen raspberries

Place all ingredients into a shaker filled with ice and shake for sixty
seconds. Double-strain into glass using a cocktail strainer and a tea
strainer, garnish with raspberries.

....

ORANGE WHITE RUSSIAN

Matt Tunnel, mixologist, Great Lakes Distillery, Milwaukee

1 oz. Rehorst Vodka, or other vodka
1 oz. Good Land Orange Liqueur, or other orange liqueur
1 oz. Good Land Coffee Liqueur, or other coffee liqueur
1½ oz. half-and-half

GLASS: rocks

Pour all ingredients into a rocks glass filled with ice. Stir once or twice.

....

"Brûléed" Banana Daiquiri (Brian West, *Alcoholmanac*)

Door County Daiquiri at Great Lakes Distillery (Great Lakes Distillery)

"BRÛLÉED" BANANA DAIQUIRI

Brian West, owner, Crucible Beverage Company

1½ oz. Great Northern Distilling Opportunity Rum, or other rum
1 oz. Giffard Banane de Bresil, or other banana liqueur
½ oz. lime juice
¼ oz. Great Northern Distilling Coffee Liqueur, or other coffee liqueur

GLASS: coupe or martini
GARNISH: thin lime wheel

Pour all ingredients into a shaker. Add ice and shake well, thirty to sixty
seconds. Strain neat into a coupe or martini glass. Garnish with a thin
lime wheel.

. . . .

DOOR COUNTY DAIQUIRI

Matt Tunnel, mixologist, Great Lakes Distillery, Milwaukee

2 oz. Roaring Dan's Rum, or other rum
¾ oz. Good Land Door County Cherry Liqueur, or other liqueur
¾ oz. lime juice
¼ oz. real maple syrup

GLASS: martini or coupe
GARNISH: cherry

Put all ingredients into a shaker filled with ice. Shake for thirty to sixty
seconds, then strain into a cocktail glass. Serve straight up with a cherry.

. . . .

CHAI SOUR

Brian Sammons, owner, Twisted Path Distillery, Milwaukee

2 oz. Twisted Path chai liqueur   ½ oz. lemon juice

GLASS: coupe or martini
GARNISH: star anise

Place all ingredients into a cocktail shaker filled with ice. Shake for thirty to sixty seconds. Strain into glass, garnish with a star anise.

. . . .

CHAI GIMLET

Brian Sammons, owner, Twisted Path Distillery, Milwaukee

2 oz. Twisted Path gin, or other gin   ¾ oz. simple syrup
¾ oz. fresh lime juice   ¼ oz. Twisted Path chai liqueur

GLASS: coupe or martini
GARNISH: lime wheel or orange peel

Place all ingredients into a cocktail shaker filled with ice. Shake for thirty to sixty seconds. Strain into glass, garnish with lime wheel or orange peel.

. . . .

BUTTERSCOTCH BLISS

Kringle Cream mixologists

2 oz. Kringle Cream liqueur   1 oz. butterscotch schnapps
1 oz. vodka   2 oz. cream soda

GLASS: martini or coupe
GARNISH: butterscotch syrup and crushed butterscotch candies

Chai Gimlet at Twisted Path Distillery (Twisted Path Distillery)

Butterscotch Bliss (Kringle Cream Liqueur)

Rim a martini or coupe glass in butterscotch syrup, then dip in crushed butterscotch candies. Set aside. Pour Kringle Cream liqueur, vodka, and schnapps into a shaker filled with ice. Shake for sixty seconds, then pour in cream soda. Stir for thirty seconds, then strain into prepared glass.

PEPPERMINT MARTINI

Kringle Cream mixologists

3 oz. Kringle Cream liqueur
½ oz. peppermint-flavored vodka

GLASS: martini or coupe
GARNISH: crushed peppermint candies and white chocolate or regular chocolate syrup

Rim a martini or coupe glass in chocolate syrup, then dip in crushed peppermint candies. Set aside. Pour Kringle cream liqueur and peppermint-flavored vodka into a shaker filled with ice. Shake for sixty seconds, then strain into prepared glass.

If you like things extra minty, add an extra ½ oz. of peppermint-flavored vodka. To make your own homemade peppermint-flavored vodka, take two cups of your favorite vodka and pour it into a mason jar. Add one cup of peppermint candies. Let sit for at least eight hours or up to overnight, strain, and serve. If you really, really like peppermint, though, you can let it sit for up to a week, but if you choose to do so, taste it once a day to prevent it from becoming overpowering.

Sex and the City and Martinis

The Cosmopolitan Martini wasn't invented for *Sex and the City*, but this cranberry-hued drink is practically synonymous with Carrie and her gal pals.

There are several different stories of the origin of this modern classic, but all of them point to it originating sometime during the late 1980s. One of the possible creators of this sweet pink drink is noted New York mixologist and barkeep Toby Cecchini, who has roots in Eau Claire (his memoir is aptly titled *Cosmopolitan*). The two most likely stories of invention are that Cecchini invented it in 1987 in New York City or that a Miami bartender in South Beach named Cheryl Cook invented it in 1985.

In any case, while it was pretty popular in the late 1980s, its popularity had waned by the early 1990s. It might have faded, except it appeared in the hands of Carrie and her gal pals during the show's second season on HBO in 1998. And suddenly, everyone, everywhere, was ordering them. Including the good folks in Wisconsin.

In Wisconsin, at the height of *SATC*'s popularity, Cosmos were served at every trendy bar and dance club, and they were often featured on Martini menus that featured other fruity and creamy vodka drinks. They soon spread to everyday taverns, bars, and supper clubs, and whole Martini menus were developed, devoted to Lemon Drop Martinis, Appletinis, and just about any fruity-flavored liqueur and vodka combination possible. But whereas the Cosmo and its cousins faded in popularity elsewhere in the country, as craft cocktails and other drinking trends took their place, the dessert Martini continues to linger in Wisconsin—and they remain popular from Green Bay to

Lake Geneva. There are supper clubs, resort hotels, and corner bars throughout the state that boast of Martini menus, and some of them have as many as thirty different flavors.

Several bartenders at Wisconsin resorts note that it's not just Wisconsinites who drink sweet Martinis here—our visitors from out-of-state like to indulge in them when they're on vacation.

"They still are quite popular here," says Elizabeth Behrens, bartender at Bar West at the Abbey Resort in Fontana. "Some of our biggest sellers are sweet Martinis. I think that when you're out at the pool or the lake, you want something sweet and refreshing."

COSMOPOLITAN

1½ oz. citrus vodka
1 oz. orange liqueur
½ oz. fresh lime juice

½ oz. simple syrup
½ oz. cranberry juice

GLASS: martini or coupe
GARNISH: fresh lemon twist

Place all ingredients in a shaker filled with ice. Shake for thirty to sixty seconds. Strain into martini or coupe glass, garnish with lemon twist.

....

GIN COSMO

1½ oz. Rehorst gin, or other gin
½ oz. Good Land cranberry liqueur
¾ oz. fresh lime juice

¾ oz. simple syrup
citrus bitters (optional)

GLASS: martini or coupe
GARNISH: Blue Jay blue cheese and extra-large dried cranberries and/or lime strip

Place all ingredients, including citrus bitters if using, in a shaker filled with ice. Shake for thirty to sixty seconds until well chilled. Strain into a martini or coupe glass.

To make garnish, slice dried cranberries not quite in half. Place small dollops of blue cheese into cranberries. If using lime strip, wrap on outside and secure with toothpick. Drop in drink or place on edge of glass.

. . . .

PRAIRIE BLOSSOM MARTINI

Corinna Todd, owner, Red Pines Bar & Grill, Onalaska

1½ oz. Ketel One peach orange blossom vodka, or other peach-flavored vodka

¾ oz. apricot liqueur

¾ oz. peach schnapps

splash of fresh orange juice, about ¼ oz.

GLASS: martini
GARNISH: orange slice

Place all ingredients in a shaker filled with ice. Shake for thirty to sixty seconds. Strain into martini glass. Garnish with orange slice.

. . . .

WISCONSIN'S LAST WORD

¾ oz. Rehorst gin, or other gin
¾ oz. Great Lakes Good Land Door County Cherry liqueur

¾ oz. green Chartreuse liqueur
¾ oz. fresh lime juice

GLASS: coupe or martini
GARNISH: dark cherry and chartreuse cheese

Place all ingredients in a shaker filled with ice. Shake for sixty seconds. Double-strain into a coupe or martini glass using a cocktail strainer and a tea strainer. Add garnish of dark cherry and chartreuse cheese.

. . . .

Acai-Tini at the Abbey Resort (Abbey Resort)

ACAI-TINI

Elizabeth Behrens, bartender, Bar West, The Abbey Resort, Lake Geneva

1 oz. Cedilla Acai Liqueur
1 oz. VeeV Acai Spirit
splash of lemon juice, about ¼ oz.
splash of simple syrup, about ¼ oz.

GLASS: martini
GARNISH: lemon twist

Combine ingredients in shaker with ice. Shake for thirty to sixty seconds or until well chilled. Strain drink into a martini glass, garnish with a lemon twist.

The Sours—Ancient Derivatives of the Old Fashioned

Sour cocktails are a bit of a misnomer—they're actually pretty sweet. They're basically a combination of booze, citrus, sugar, and maybe a little water. As such, they're versions of alcoholic punch, which predates the original cocktail (which is the traditional Old Fashioned, made without citrus but with bitters), and they're some of the most historic cocktails out there.

Not only that, but they have a long history here in Wisconsin. Now, the first written (that we know of) reference to a sour comes from Toronto, on a written list of available cocktails in 1856 at a bar called Mart Ackerman's Saloon. Six years later, the first recipe was recorded in Jerry Thomas's historic book *The Bartender's Guide* (1862). Thomas has three basic recipes for a sour—a Brandy Sour, a Gin Sour, and something called the Santa Cruz, which is basically a Rum Sour (a Daiquiri, really).

But whiskey, as in Whiskey Sour, didn't show up in print until 1870, and the very first written reference to a Whiskey Sour was from the January 4 edition of that year's *Waukesha Plain Dealer*. That's right: the very first Whiskey Sour mention comes from Waukesha. Terrence McGrant writes of playing billiards and drinking with his cousin and another guy, referred to as a Methodist from Galena, Illinois. "'Then may God have mercy on your soul,' says I, taking a drink out of me cousin's glass. 'Amen' says the Methodist, as he ordered another whisky sour."

This very casual reference to the drink, without any explanation, reveals that everybody understood what it was. A few years later, in 1884, the *Milwaukee Journal* published a poem entitled "The Busy Bar-tender," and the first few lines were:

> How doth the busy bar-tender
> Improve each shining hour,
> Drawing lager from the keg
> Or mixing whisky sour.

In 1888, a *Milwaukee Journal* reporter tagged along with a political candidate, Mr. Hoard. Hoard left a political event with his cronies, and then they "marched by a devious route to the Milwaukee Club. There a light and simple repast, consisting of a whisky-sour, a whisky cock-tail and a cigar . . . was partaken." Hoard, the reporter noted, was not a Prohibitionist.

Sours, whether they're of the whiskey, gin, or brandy variety, continued up to Prohibition, during Prohibition, and then after Prohibition to the present. Like many other drinks in Wisconsin, especially after Prohibition, they tend to skew sweeter here, and corner taverns that don't make their own sour mix simply top a shot or two of whiskey with sour soda.

But a properly made sour is made with real citrus juice—lemon, lime, and/or grapefruit—along with sugar or simple syrup or another sweetener such as honey, maple syrup, or agave. And while it's sweet, it's balanced, and it's a perfectly refreshing drink for summer.

Twisted Palmer at Twisted Path Distillery
(Twisted Path Distillery)

TWISTED PALMER

Brian Sammons, owner, Twisted Path Distillery, Milwaukee

1½ oz. Twisted Path vodka, or other vodka

1½ oz. fresh lemon juice

1½ oz. simple syrup

2 oz. unsweetened iced tea

5 large mint leaves

GLASS: pint or Collins
GARNISH: lemon wheel or wedge and mint sprig

Pour all ingredients together in a shaker filled with ice. Shake for thirty to sixty seconds, strain into a pint or Collins glass filled with ice, and garnish with lemon wheel or wedge and mint sprig.

PALOMA

bartending staff at Movida Restaurant, Milwaukee

1½ oz. El Jimador Blanco tequila, or other tequila
¼ oz. fresh lime juice
4 to 6 oz. Jaritos grapefruit soda

GLASS: rocks
GARNISH: salt and Tajin seasoning, dehydrated grapefruit slice, and tarragon sprig

Pour tequila and lime juice into a rocks glass that has already been rimmed with salt and Tajin seasoning (mix an equal amount of salt and seasoning onto a plate, rub a lime wedge around the rim, then dip into the mixture). Add ice, then top with grapefruit soda, and garnish with dehydrated grapefruit slice and sprig of tarragon.

....

BLACKBERRY MINT WHISKEY SOUR

Michele Price, caterer and food blogger,
appetiteforentertaining.com, Hales Corners

3 fresh blackberries
2 fresh mint leaves
1½ oz. Kinnickinnic Whiskey, or other whiskey
4 to 6 oz. sour soda

GLASS: old fashioned or rocks
GARNISH: fresh blackberries and mint

Place the blackberries and mint leaves at the bottom of the glass and muddle gently until the blackberries are broken down. Add ice, whiskey, and sour soda. Garnish with fresh blackberries and a sprig of mint.

....

Paloma at Movida Restaurant (Stand Eat Drink)

Blackberry Mint Whiskey Sour (Appetite for Entertaining)

Summer Delight at Hatch Distilling Co. (Kyle Edwards)

WHISKEY SOUR

Nathan Greenwalt, owner, Old Sugar Distillery, Madison

1 sugar cube
splash of water, about ¼ to ½ oz.
2 lime wedges
1¾ oz. Queen Jennie Sorghum Whiskey, or other whiskey

GLASS: rocks or old fashioned
GARNISH: maraschino cherry

In a rocks glass, muddle the sugar with a small splash of water until the sugar is mostly dissolved. Add lime wedges and continue to muddle until sugar is dissolved and lime oils are extracted. Add whiskey, stir, and top with ice. Garnish with a maraschino cherry.

. . . .

SUMMER DELIGHT

Jessica Hatch, bar manager, Hatch Distilling Co., Egg Harbor

½ oz. simple syrup
3 to 4 basil leaves
2 strawberries
4 cucumber-slice quarters
1½ oz. Hatch gin, or other gin
4 oz. Sprite

GLASS: old fashioned or rocks
GARNISH: cucumber wheel and basil leaves

Gently muddle syrup, basil, strawberries, and cucumbers together. Top with gin and ice, stir, then top with Sprite. Garnish with cucumber wheel and basil.

. . . .

ISLAND TIME

Robin Ditello, owner, Nelsen's Hall, Washington Island

1½ oz. Pinnacle tropical punch vodka, or other flavored vodka

2 dashes Blue Curaçao, about ¼ oz.

2 dashes Midori, or other melon liqueur, about ¼ oz.

3 to 4 oz. sweet soda

3 to 4 oz. sour soda

GLASS: Collins or rocks

Pour vodka into a pint glass filled with ice. Dash Blue Curaçao and Midori on top, then fill with half sweet soda and half sour soda.

....

A Shot and a Beer

We don't only drink our whiskey in sours or Old Fashioneds. We also drink our whiskey straight. And most often, with a beer chaser. Related to the history of the Bloody Mary beer chaser is the history of the shot and a beer. (This is sometimes called a Boilermaker, but that's when the beer is served first and the whiskey is served second, and sometimes the whiskey is dropped into the beer. Otherwise, it's often just called a shot and a beer.) While other states served whiskey with a water back, here in Wisconsin we've served whiskey, vodka, gin, etc., with a beer chaser.

The term "beer chaser" or "a shot and a beer" dates back at least to the early twentieth century. I found several references in old newspapers referring to men (but sometimes women) drinking whiskey and sipping beer chasers. They were all references in passing, as if it were a regular occurrence.

By the 1930s it was so common that it was referred to in police reports. A waitress served a man a whiskey and a beer chaser at the Krazy Kat bar in Milwaukee, but then the guy stuck his hand in the cash register, swiping seventeen dollars. The story, which ran in the *Milwaukee Sentinel* on December 18, 1937, indicates the waitress was peeved, especially since he hadn't paid for his drink before stealing the money.

In 1942, a ticked-off Milwaukee resident, who only signed his letter to the *Milwaukee Journal* "S. R.," suggested rationing alcohol because of its societal ills. "And tavern customers should be rationed to a shot and a beer a day."

The shot could be anything, but in the past and even today it's most often whiskey. Tripper Duval, who used to work for a distribution company and today is co-owner of the Lost Whale in Milwaukee, says that one of the most interesting things he learned about Wisconsin drinking habits is that northern Wisconsin is a testing ground for national whiskey brands, particularly rye. "I don't know why that is," Duval says.

In any case, Wisconsin continues to drink plenty of whiskey, shots and otherwise, and sometimes shots get dunked straight into beer.

That's the case at Ashling on the Lough in Kenosha, where Ireland's most famous beer, Guinness, gets gussied up with everything from vanilla to raspberry liqueurs. Wisconsin isn't the only spot on the globe that takes its beer with a shot. Ireland, of course, has a long history of Guinness and a shot of whiskey, and while you can definitely order a pint of Guinness and a shot of Irish whiskey at Ashling, you can also have some innovative twists on this traditional Irish combination.

Ramos Guin(ness) Fizz (Brian West, *Alcoholmanac*)

CARAMEL DELIGHT

Paul Ward, general manager, Ashling on the Lough, Kenosha

1½ oz. caramel liqueur
8 oz. Guinness

GLASS: pint or Collins

Pour Guinness into a glass, top with liqueur. Stir and enjoy.

Other variations to change up the profile of the cocktail: substitute the caramel liqueur with chocolate liqueur, Bailey's liqueur, Chambord raspberry liqueur, espresso liqueur, or vanilla vodka.

. . . .

RAMOS GUIN(NESS) FIZZ

Ryan Williams, first printed by Brian West in *Alcoholmanac*, 2016

1½ oz. Ron Zacapa twenty-three-year-old rum, or other rum
¾ oz. lemon juice
1 oz. vanilla simple syrup
1 oz. 4× Guinness reduction
2 oz. heavy cream
1 egg white
3 dashes Bittercube Blackstrap bitters, or other bitters
4 oz. Guinness, divided
2 drops orange blossom water

GLASS: goblet
GARNISH: orange peel

Add all ingredients together, except 4 oz. Guinness and orange blossom water, in shaking tin. Add one 1-inch cubic ice cube (Kold Draft ice if you have it) and "dry" shake until cube has melted. (A dry shake is shaking the ingredients without ice, or, in this case, with a single cube).

Then add fresh ice and shake for an additional minute (called a standard wet shake). To serve, pour 2 oz. Guinness in bottom of goblet, add ice, then double-strain cocktail (using a cocktail strainer and a tea strainer) on top of Guinness, then top with an additional 2 oz. Guinness. Place 2 drops of orange blossom water and orange peel in the middle of the top of the drink and serve with a long straw.

To make the vanilla simple syrup, split one Madagascar vanilla bean pod in half lengthwise, and steep in 10 oz. of hot water. After ten minutes, strain and add an equal amount of granulated sugar by mass (approximately 296 grams or about 1¼ cups) and stir until fully dissolved.

To make the 4× Guinness reduction, empty one can of Guinness into a medium-size pot and place on a stovetop set to medium-low heat. Heat the beer at the lowest possible temperature while still allowing beer to evaporate. Be careful not to let it become too hot and hit a rolling boil, or else you will caramelize the beer and get an unwanted burnt taste. Remove from stovetop after losing approximately 75 percent of volume and let cool.

....

Stubborn Mules

"Did you talk about the Mule yet?" asks Corinna Todd, owner of the Red Pines Bar & Grill in Onalaska. "They are so popular."

The Moscow Mule—renamed, in some cases, the Milwaukee or Madison Mule at various bars in both cities—actually started in the 1940s in Los Angeles. It was invented at the Cock 'n Bull British pub, and it was basically invented by a bartender and/or owner to clean out the bar's stock of both ginger beer and vodka. Add in some lime juice, serve it in a copper cup, and it was a hit—back when Americans didn't really drink much vodka.

It started resurging in popularity in 2016, and here in Wisconsin its popularity continues, strong as ever. "The Mule and the Old Fashioned are the top-selling cocktails in our tasting room," says Evan Hughes, who co-owns Central Standard Distillery in Milwaukee with Pat McQuillan. Besides the regular Mule, they also serve one made with their Door County cherry vodka. A version of their Mule, called the Wisconsin Mule, is served at Miller Park, and besides their vodka, it's made with Top Note's ginger beer.

MOSCOW MULE

½ oz. fresh lime juice
1½ oz. vodka
4 to 6 oz. ginger beer

GLASS: copper mug
GARNISH: lime wheel

Squeeze fresh lime juice into mug. Top with vodka, add an ice cube or two, stir, then top with ginger beer and garnish with a lime wheel.

. . . .

APPLE BUTTER BOURBON FIZZ
Door County Distillery, Sturgeon Bay

3 tbsp. apple butter
2 oz. Door County Distillery Bourbon, or other bourbon
dash cinnamon
4 to 6 oz. ginger beer

GLASS: rocks
GARNISH: cinnamon or cinnamon-and-sugar mix, cinnamon sticks

Wipe a lemon around the rim of a rocks glass. Dip glass into cinnamon or cinnamon-and-sugar mix. Set aside. Add apple butter, bourbon, and dash of cinnamon to a shaker filled with ice. Shake for thirty to sixty seconds, then strain into prepared rocks glass. Top with ginger beer, garnish with cinnamon sticks.

....

A Bitter History

Wisconsin consumes more Angostura bitters than any other state. Part of that has to do with our Old Fashioned tradition: a properly made Wisconsin Old Fashioned, whether it's served sweet or sour, made with brandy or whiskey, always, always has bitters in it, and the traditional bitters of choice for an Old Fashioned is Angostura. If you don't have bitters, the cocktail doesn't taste the same. Years ago, when I was interviewing Doug Mackenzie and Jason Neu, back when both of them worked at Great Lakes Distillery, Neu made me two Old Fashioneds—one with bitters, and one without—and the one without just tasted bland.

But our craving for Old Fashioneds isn't why we consume so much Angostura. The reason is we actually drink bitters straight.

And that gets us to the bitters club at Nelsen's Hall on Washington Island. Nelsen's Hall (now known as Nelsen's Hall Bitters Pub) was originally a dance hall opened by Tom Nelsen in 1899. Three years later, he added the bar, and then, in 1920, Prohibition hit. But Nelsen was an enterprising man, and rather than close he got himself a pharmaceutical license to sell bitters. Actual doctors could prescribe alcohol, and Nelsen was not a doctor. But bitters were classified as a stomach tonic, and you didn't need a medical license to sell them.

Nelsen sold the bitters—as shots—and even though the Feds

did try to shutter his doors, they never were able to, which is why Nelsen's is the oldest continuously operated bar in the state. After repeal, the shots of bitters continued as an island tradition, and eventually Nelsen's nephew and his wife (who took over the pub from him) established a Bitters Club. The Bitters Club has continued to this day, and if you join the club—by downing a shot of bitters—you get to sign the guest book (there are hundreds lining the bar's shelves) and you get a certificate.

Robin Ditello and Douglas Delaporte are the bar's seventh owners. The bar serves up thousands upon thousands of shots of bitters every year. "Nobody can come close to us," Ditello says.

Ditello frequently gets approached by other bitters makers, but other bitters don't taste the same as Angostura, she says. Like the original Nelsen, Ditello enjoys a daily shot of bitters. People who drink a shot of bitters either love it

A plaque at Nelsen's Hall
(Kyle Edwards)

or hate it, she says. Chances are, if you have stomach problems, you might not enjoy it—it is a tonic, after all.

Visitors who sign the bitters book often write comments like "Over the teeth, past the gums, watch out stomach, here it comes!!" Or, "My hair is growing back." Even better, "Almost as good as a shot of pickle juice."

"You have to like bitters to work here," Ditello says, adding that bitters are used in plenty of the cocktails and a few of the dishes. But most of the bitters go into shots, which get lined up in rows on busy nights, and that's just how it should be.

SPRING CHAMPAGNE COCKTAIL

Jeff Kinder, bar manager, Jazz Estate, Milwaukee

7 dashes lavender bitters blend
sugar cube
6 oz. dry sparkling wine or champagne

GLASS: champagne flute
GARNISH: lemon zest

Place a sugar cube into a flute. Place seven dashes of bitters onto the sugar cube. Fill with sparkling wine, garnish with lemon zest.

To make lavender bitters blend, combine 1 oz. Scrappy's Lavender Bitters, 1 oz. Peychaud's Bitters, and ½ oz. Giffard's vanilla de Madagascar.

....

The Green Fairy: Or, Absinthe in Wisconsin

Guy Rehorst made history in 2004 when he opened up the very first distillery in the state of Wisconsin since Prohibition. And he continued to make history, as he changed laws (becoming the first distillery to be allowed to have visitors taste his product in an actual tasting room) and forged new traditions.

One of the newfangled things he did was make absinthe. Absinthe, which contains wormwood and derives its name from the Latin *absinthium*, which means wormwood, was banned in 1912 because it was believed to have hallucinogenic properties. In reality, the chemical thujone, which wormwood contains and which can cause hallucinations, is present in such small amounts in absinthe that it doesn't cause hallucinations.

In any case, it was banned, and the ban didn't get lifted until 2007. In 2009, Rehorst began making absinthe in Milwaukee. He started with two nineteenth-century recipes, making Amerique 1912 Absinthe Verte and Amerique 1912 Absinthe Rouge. The verte is a traditional green absinthe, and the rouge is a red absinthe, which gets its lovely hue from hibiscus. Rehorst also began making a black absinthe, Amerique 1912 Blacksinthe (Absinthe Noir) in 2017, using catechu bark to naturally color it. Its bottles are also pretty cool, and if you have a blacklight up for Halloween, they glow.

But while Rehorst was groundbreaking in making absinthe—he was one of the very first distilleries in the country to make it after the ban was lifted—he wasn't the first person to ever make absinthe in Wisconsin. That honor belongs to Leander Drew, a doctor in Sauk County. Drew, a graduate of Dartmouth College, moved his family to Wisconsin in 1848, and he started the very first distillery in Wisconsin.

Like many doctors of his era, he mixed his own medicines. He grew wormwood and distilled it for medicinal purposes. After he passed away in 1858, his son, another L. S. Drew, continued the production of wormwood—so much, in fact, that he earned the nickname "Wormwood" Drew. A story published in the *L'Abeille de la Nouvelle-Orleans* paper in 1902 described him thus: "This queer husbandman bears the unique distinction of being the greatest producer and of having the most extensive wormwood works in the United States, if not in the world."

Rehorst says that the climate of Wisconsin is exceptionally good for growing wormwood. "We grow some out on our patio here at the distillery," he says.

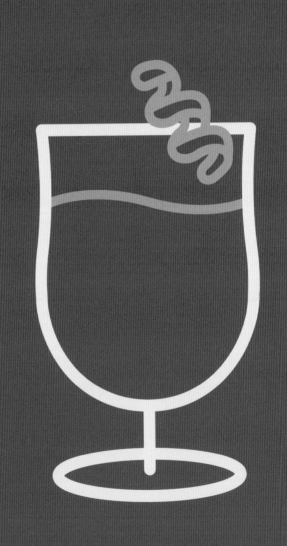

N°7

NEW WISCONSIN COCKTAILS

OTHER DRINKS THAT AIM TO PUT THE DAIRY STATE ON THE COCKTAIL MAP

FOR EVERY BARTENDER WHO PUTS A SIGNATURE TWIST ON A BRANDY OLD FASHIONED, THERE'S ANOTHER BARTENDER WHO'S TRYING TO CREATE A NEW COCKTAIL THAT EVERYONE WILL START CLAMORING FOR. IT'S THE DREAM OF MANY MIXOLOGISTS TO CREATE A NEW DRINK THAT BECOMES A CLASSIC COCKTAIL, AND WISCONSIN'S TALENTED BARTENDERS ARE REGULARLY BEING RECOGNIZED IN NATIONAL AND INTERNATIONAL COMPETITIONS.

But more than that, they are recognized at home—in the bars and restaurants where they work—because people keep coming back for those cocktails they can't get anyplace else. Scotty McCormick, head bartender at Lola's Restaurant at The Osthoff Resort in Elkhart Lake, says that good cocktails create "When Harry Met Sally" moments—once someone sees the cocktail, others "will have what she's having." "You never sell just one," McCormick says.

Here are some of these delicious cocktails—and some of the stories behind their creation—that might just be good enough to become new classics, perhaps even exported to other states.

The Way of the Phoenix

Adam Sarkis put Braise restaurant's Milwaukee bar on the map when he was in charge of the menu. He went on to open the Phoenix Cocktail Club, took his pop-up tiki–Shaquille O'Neal bar (called the

Loveshaq) to bars across the country, and this Door County native has moved south, to Chicago, where he is the general manager of the Waydown Bar at the Ace Hotel.

Sarkis, who was originally a filmmaker, says that the King's Way has one key element of a modern classic cocktail: all the ingredients can be found on hand at most bars and restaurants.

"I spent three years [at Braise] trying to come up with a modern classic. We wanted to invent a modern drink that no one had ever seen but would be made with bottles that were on almost everyone's back bar," says Sarkis. "We played around with different ingredients and different ratios, and we made a bunch of bad drinks."

Once he moved to open the Phoenix Cocktail Club, the owner there, Robert King, loved cognac, so Sarkis put this cocktail together for him. "I made that drink, and he says 'Ooh, I want another one of those,'" Sarkis says. "I spent a couple of years trying to make something like this, and it happened kind of by accident."

Later, after naming the cocktail after King and putting it on the menu, Sarkis says he found only one recipe that was slightly similar in an old book of Hennesey's cocktails, but it's not the same.

THE KING'S WAY

2 oz. Hennessey or Remy Martin, or other cognac of brandy
¾ oz. fresh lemon juice
½ oz. Campari

½ oz. honey simple syrup
2 dashes orange bitters

GLASS: martini or coupe
GARNISH: orange zest

Place all ingredients in cocktail shaker filled with ice. Shake for at least sixty seconds, then strain into cocktail glass. Garnish with orange zest.

You can make this cocktail with regular simple syrup, but Sarkis says "it tastes better with honey syrup." Honey simple syrup can be made by combining ½ cup honey honey and ¼ cup hot water. Stir honey and water together until honey is completely dissolved in water.

....

Another cocktail that Sarkis took with him to Chicago is The Million Dollar Daiquiri. "I get butterflies in my stomach every time someone orders one," Sarkis says.

The drink is basically taking a French 75—a champagne, simple syrup, lemon juice, and gin cocktail—and seeing if you could put a different drink inside of it. So Sarkis took a rum Daiquiri and put it inside that cocktail, then replaced the champagne with dry sparkling rosé.

THE MILLION DOLLAR DAIQUIRI, THE PHOENIX VERSION

2 oz. white rum
¾ oz. simple syrup
¾ oz. lime juice
1½ oz. sparkling dry rosé

GLASS: coupe or martini

Shake all ingredients, except wine, with ice for ten to twenty seconds, then double-strain it into a stemmed coupe or martini glass using a cocktail strainer and a tea strainer. Top with rosé.

....

THE MILLION DOLLAR DAIQUIRI, THE CHICAGO VERSION

1½ oz. white rum
½ oz. amontillado sherry
¾ oz. simple syrup
¾ oz. lime juice
1½ oz. sparkling dry rosé

GLASS: coupe or martini

Shake all ingredients, except wine, with ice for ten to twenty seconds, then double-strain it into a stemmed coupe or martini glass using a cocktail strainer and a tea strainer. Top with rosé.

....

Locally Sourced Inspirations

Katie Wysocki says she and her staff at the Devon Seafood + Steak restaurant in Glendale love creating signature cocktails for guests, and it's not just the bartenders on staff who come up with the recipes—servers and chefs do, too—and any signature cocktail on the menu is labeled with the name of its creator.

"They really create this experience for guests," Wysocki says. "It creates a memory, and it is something that they can't get anywhere else."

Wysocki was experimenting with a brandy made by Wollersheim, and she was planning to use Great Lakes Distillery's orange liqueur, Good Land. "I love sidecars, personally, but I wanted to create a version made with just Wisconsin ingredients," she says. "Our [liquor] rep came in one day and said 'Hey, we've got this new cranberry liqueur,'" Wysocki says. "I said 'That's a cool idea.'"

Not only was it an intriguing concept but Wysocki liked the way Good Land's cranberry played better in the cocktail than its orange. "It adds just the right amount of tart crispness to the cocktail, and it was a winner," she says.

THE SCONNIE SIDECAR

Katie Wysocki, general manager, Devon Seafood + Steak, Glendale

1 oz. Wollersheim brandy, or other brandy
1 oz. Good Land cranberry liqueur
¾ oz. lemon juice
½ oz. simple syrup
1 lime wedge

GLASS: coupe or martini
GARNISH: lime and cranberry flag

Pour brandy, cranberry liqueur, lemon juice, and simple syrup into a shaker filled with ice. Squeeze juice from lime wedge into the mixture. Shake for thirty to sixty seconds, then strain into glass. Garnish with lime and cranberry flag.

A flag is usually an orange wedge wrapped around a cherry, but in this case it's a lime wedge wrapped around a fresh cranberry.

Wysocki does her best to mentor her staff, and her bartenders aren't the only ones at Devon who come up with interesting and intriguing drinks. Another signature cocktail on the menu was created by server Melissa Jackson. The drink, The Jackson 5, has five ingredients, and Jackson created it.

Sconnie Sidecar at Devon Seafood + Steak (Devon Seafood + Steak)

THE JACKSON 5

Melissa Jackson, server, Devon Seafood + Steak, Glendale

2 oz. Koval 4 Grain whiskey, or other whiskey
1 oz. cranberry juice
¾ oz. simple syrup
1 lime wedge
3 blackberries

GLASS: coupe or martini
GARNISH: lime and additional blackberries

Muddle lime and blackberries with simple syrup in the bottom of a shaker. Top with whiskey and cranberry juice, shake, then double-strain into a coupe or martini glass using a cocktail strainer and a tea strainer. Garnish with additional lime and blackberries.

A Taste of Nepal

People from all over Wisconsin and as far away as Minnesota and Illinois travel to Thiensville to enjoy Barkha Daily's Nepalese cuisine at her restaurant, The Cheel. Daily and her husband, Jesse, had been involved with the local Thiensville Farmers' Market, and whenever she promoted the market, she would cook meals using farm-fresh ingredients in her family's recipes—and spices sent by her mother from Nepal. Every time she cooked a special meal, people asked her when she was going to open her own restaurant, so finally she and her husband opened The Cheel in 2014. In 2018, they added the Baaree beer garden, and their cocktails are just as inventive as their cuisine.

One of the reasons for the inventive cocktails is that Drew Kassner, general manager and head mixologist, often teams up with Barkha and other staff members to come up with traditional Wisconsin and classic cocktails, but with a Nepalese twist. If you want to make good cocktails at home, Kassner advises, "Always make your own simple syrup, and always make your own sour mix, using fresh juices."

For basic simple syrup, Kassner advises using equal parts hot water and sugar, but then you can mix things up by adding spices, herbs, and juices. Kassner makes several different syrups in-house, infuses spirits, and even smokes some of his juices. Daily also has her mother send her spices direct from Nepal, and they toast and grind the spices before using them in both food and beverages. "It's really a collaboration," Kassner says, of the new cocktails. "This restaurant is very chef-driven, and I'm always asking our chefs and our servers, 'What do you think of this?'"

Katmandu 75 at The Cheel

While each of The Cheel's syrups listed below (and in chapter 8) is used in specific recipes, they can also be used for regular Old Fashioneds, sours, and other classic cocktails, giving them a distinctive twist. Daily says that they can be used to marinate meats and vegetables, too.

KATMANDU 75

Drew Kassner, general manager and head mixologist,
The Cheel, Thiensville

1 oz. Rehorst gin, or other gin
¾ oz. fresh lemon juice
½ oz. rosemary simple syrup
½ oz. Domaine de Canton ginger liqueur, or other ginger liqueur
1 dropper of Bittercube Jamaica No. 1 bitters, or other bitters
2 oz. Spanish cava, or other dry sparkling wine

GLASS: coupe or rocks
GARNISH: rosemary sprig and dried lemon wheel

Place all ingredients, except cava, into a shaker filled with ice. Shake for ten seconds, strain into coupe or rocks glass, top with cava and garnishes.

Rosemary simple syrup can be made by putting 2 cups hot water, 2 cups sugar, 4 rosemary sprigs (stems removed), and ¼ tsp. salt into a blender. Blend until smooth, then strain.

· ·

SPICED YETI

Drew Kassner, general manager and head mixologist,
The Cheel, Thiensville

2 oz. Rehorst vodka, or other vodka

1 oz. spiced simple syrup

¾ oz. fresh lemon juice

1 full dropper Bittercube Jamaican
No. 2 bitters, or other bitters

2 oz. seltzer

GLASS: coupe
GARNISH: dehydrated lemon wheel

Place all ingredients, except seltzer, in a shaker filled with ice. Shake for
about ten seconds, strain into a chilled coupe glass, top with seltzer,
and garnish with dehydrated lemon wheel. Kassner says that cognac
could replace the vodka for an entirely different yet equally refreshing
cocktail.

The easiest way to make spiced simple syrup is to toast spices—1 stick
cinnamon, 1 tsp. black cardamom, 1 tsp. green cardamom, ½ tsp. ground
cloves, ½ tsp. black peppercorns—over medium-high heat until fragrant,
then grind. Whisk ground spices, 1 cup hot water, 1 cup honey, and
1 cup sugar together until sugar is dissolved, then strain. Daily says that
this syrup is amazing for a red meat marinade, and it can be added to
slushes, too.

....

DOWN IN MEXICO

Drew Kassner, general manager and head mixologist,
The Cheel, Thiensville

1½ oz. silver tequila or mezcal

½ oz. Rothman Winter Orchard liqueur, or other apricot liqueur

½ oz. simple syrup

¾ oz. hickory smoked lemon juice

GLASS: rocks
GARNISH: salt and lemon peel twisted on a toothpick

Shake all ingredients together until well chilled, about thirty seconds. Strain into prepared rocks glass (lemon wedge wiped around the edge, rimmed in salt) filled with ice. Top with a lemon peel twisted around a toothpick.

To make hickory smoked lemon juice, grill the lemon halves (at least two, more if you want to prepare a larger batch) until they are charred. Then put them in an electric smoker with hickory smoke for about thirty minutes. Remove, let cool, then juice. "If you tried to smoke the lemons without grilling them, they wouldn't pick up enough of the smoke," Kassner says. "The smoking softens the acidity." Daily points out that this, too, is a great marinade.

....

Summer Loving

Scotty McCormick's boss at Lola's tasked him with coming up with a summer drink that customers could enjoy on the patio. The thing is, when things get busy at the Osthoff Resort, bartenders get swamped— so the cocktail couldn't be complicated, it couldn't require a lot of fancy ingredients, and it definitely couldn't involve any time-intensive preparations. So McCormick came up with the Green Goose. "It's very simple to make, but visually it's phenomenal," he says. "It doesn't need an umbrella or all that crap. Selling one sells itself. It's like a Brandy Alexander ice cream drink, people watch it go by, and then they order one. If you saw one of these cocktails go out, you would probably order one just to try it, or you're going to at least inquire about it."

Green Goose at Osthoff Resort

THE GREEN GOOSE

1½ oz. Grey Goose vodka, or other vodka

½ oz. Midori, or other melon liqueur

2 to 3 oz. Sprite, or other white soda or seltzer

1 lime wedge

GLASS: rocks

GARNISH: cucumber wheel and lime wedge

Pour vodka and Midori into the bottom of a rocks glass, top with ice,
fill with soda or seltzer. Squeeze lime wedge into top of drink. Garnish
with cucumber wheel and fresh lime wedge. And after squeezing or
not squeezing the additional lime into the cocktail (it's the customer's
choice, McCormick says), put the cucumber into the drink, then enjoy it
as a crisp treat after you're finished sipping the cocktail.

. . . .

Other Great Wisconsin Cocktails from the Volumes of the *Alcoholmanac*

For eleven years, Brian West and his wife published the *Alcoholmanac* magazine in Milwaukee, highlighting the great work of Milwaukee and Wisconsin bartenders. In 2018, he took a hiatus from publishing the magazine to focus on his new project, Crucible Beverage Company. "The idea comes from melting down metals to form alloys, which are in theory stronger than the original metals," West says. "Maybe your company isn't large enough to have someone in marketing, but maybe you can co-opt my time with a number of different brands to promote your product in Milwaukee and Madison."

West still believes in championing bartenders and great bar products, and he believes our Wisconsin cocktail culture and bartenders can stand up to any of the best in the country. Here are a couple of innovative recipes that still resonate with West.

WHITE NEGRONI

CocktailDudes, first published in *Alcoholmanac,* 2015

1½ oz. Plymouth gin, or other gin
1 oz. Cocchi Americano, or other white vermouth
1 oz. Salers Aperitif, or other apertif

GLASS: coupe
GARNISH: long swath of orange peel

Add all ingredients, with ice, to a mixing glass. Stir to chill and strain into a coupe glass. Garnish with a long orange swath.

White Negroni (Brian West, *Alcoholmanac*)

An Old Fashioned Cuban Revolver
(Brian West, *Alcoholmanac*)

AN OLD FASHIONED CUBAN REVOLVER

Brian West, developed in a cocktail workshop with several
Milwaukee bartenders, first published in *Alcoholmanac*, 2017

1½ oz. Great Northern Distilling Opportunity Rum, or other rum

½ oz. Good Land orange liqueur, or other orange liqueur

¼ oz. Fernet Branca Menta

¼ oz. cold-brew simple syrup

¼ oz. cold-brew coffee

GLASS: old fashioned or rocks
GARNISH: orange peel

Combine ingredients into a mixing glass with ice. Stir rapidly until
diluted and cold. Strain over fresh ice into an old fashioned glass.
Garnish with an orange peel, oils expressed over the drink.

Cold-brew simple syrup can be made by combining equal parts
cold-brew coffee and white cane sugar in a saucepan. Bring to simmer,
stirring constantly until sugar is completely dissolved. Remove
from heat and allow to cool. Store in a heat-resistant container and
refrigerate between uses.

Cocktail Competitions

In 2019, Central Standard Distillery held its first-ever cocktail competition: 86'D, at Vogel Hall in Milwaukee. The competition was modeled after the *Chopped* television program in which chefs had to make dishes on the spot using secret ingredients. At this particular competition, there were three different rounds. In one round, contestants had to use pickled cherries and egg, in another they had to use sesame oil. And in one round, they had to use cotton candy, kiwano melon, and hibiscus tea leaves. "Some of the stuff they came up with was pretty impressive," says Evan Hughes, cofounder of the distillery. "People were really blown away."

"It was a ton of fun," adds Pat McQuillan, distillery cofounder.

The clear winner of all three rounds was Paul Oenig, who came up with three different, unusual cocktails, including a pretty spectacular, eye-catching one called the Cotton Canary.

COTTON CANARY

Paul Oenig, mixologist, Phoenix Club, Milwaukee

2 oz. Central Standard Cabernet-finished bourbon, or other bourbon, infused with Rishi Tea hibiscus berry tea
¾ oz. Domaine de Canton ginger liqueur, or other ginger liqueur
¾ oz. fresh lemon juice
⅞ oz. simple syrup
3 dashes Angostura bitters, or other bitters
1 dash orange bitters
1 dash chocolate bitters
pinch of black sea salt

GLASS: coupe
GARNISH: slice of kiwano or other tropical melon, lemon wedge, grapefruit wedge, tuft of cotton candy

To quickly infuse the tea into the drink, place 1 to 2 tsp. dry Rishi hibiscus berry tea into a cocktail shaker along with bourbon, ginger liqueur, lemon juice, simple syrup, the three different bitters, and sea salt. (Alternatively, steep five sachets of tea per 750 ml of bourbon for one to two days.) Shake vigorously with ice. Double-strain into a glass using a cocktail strainer and a tea strainer, place thin slice of melon on top. Squeeze lemon and grapefruit wedges into drink. Add tuft of cotton candy just before serving.

Cotton Canary (Central Standard Craft Distillery)

Bartending Lessons

Once a month at the Palomino Bar and Grill in Milwaukee's trendy Bayview neighborhood, a group of enthusiasts gather to learn more about making cocktails from Aubrey Dodd, a mixologist from Badger Liquor. Sometimes she is the only instructor, and sometimes she brings in distillery reps or owners so her students can meet the people who are making the spirits.

But no matter the subject—whether it's Margaritas or Old Fashioneds—usually bar manager Jordan Garris is on hand. And the way Dodd always starts the class is to make introductions with a welcome cocktail, which Garris expertly prepares.

One of her most popular classes—which she's taught throughout the state—is on the difference between Wisconsin Old Fashioneds and traditional Old Fashioneds. At this particular class, Garris introduced students to another booze-forward cocktail, this time a sort of savory berry and basil twist on the Whiskey Sour, another very popular Wisconsin drink.

SUBTLY NUMB
Jordan Garris, bar manager, Palomino Bar and Grill, Milwaukee

2 oz. Central Standard bourbon, or other bourbon
¼ oz. Cocchi Americano, or other vermouth
¼ oz. Apologue Aronia berry liqueur, or other berry liqueur
½ oz. basil simple syrup
¼ oz. lemon juice
1 dash whiskey barrel–aged bitters

GLASS: rocks

Pour all ingredients into a shaker filled with ice. Shake for thirty to sixty seconds, then double-strain into a rocks glass filled with ice using a cocktail strainer and a tea strainer.

To make basil simple syrup, combine one cup water and one cup sugar, plus a large handful of basil, into a saucepan and heat over medium heat, stirring frequently until sugar is completely dissolved. Remove from heat and let cool completely. Remove basil and use.

....

The Art of the Cocktail

At the Saint Kate Arts Hotel in Milwaukee, the art isn't found only on the walls or in the rooms. It's also found in each of the very carefully curated cocktails. One such summery cocktail is Millions of Peaches. If you don't want to take the time to make it, it's served on draft at the Bar at Saint Kate's.

MILLIONS OF PEACHES

Josh Stender, beverage director, Saint Kate Arts Hotel, Milwaukee

1½ oz. Rehorst vodka, or other vodka
¾ oz. fresh lemon juice
¾ oz. champagne honey simple syrup
¼ oz. Mathilde Peche, or other peach liqueur
2 dashes Bittercube Bolivar bitters, or other bitters

GLASS: rocks
GARNISH: bee pollen, dried lavender, and dehydrated blood orange wheel

Millions of Peaches at Saint Kate Arts Hotel

Pour all ingredients into a shaker filled with ice. Shake for thirty to sixty seconds, then strain into glass filled with ice. Add garnishes and serve.

To make champagne syrup, bring two to three cups champagne to a boil, then reduce the heat to medium-low and cook until the champagne becomes a syrupy consistency. Then, make a honey syrup by combining equal parts honey and hot water, stirring until the honey is dissolved. To make the champagne honey syrup, combine equal parts champagne syrup with honey syrup.

....

Kohler Cocktails

The AAA Five Diamond-rated American Club in Kohler is known for its annual Kohler Food & Wine Experience, in which famed and fabled chefs and winemakers from around the world gather to teach classes and mingle with foodies. It's a who's who of wine and food, but what most people might not know about the event is that it also pulls in mixologists and spirits companies from across the country. (It's also worth noting that Kohler is a company that specializes in toilets and booze, which has to be a Wisconsin thing.)

One of the most talented mixologists, who is always at the event, is Kohler's very own Peter Kalleward. Kalleward was part of the team that helped develop Kohler Dark Chocolate Brandy with Central Standard Distillery, and he uses both the original chocolate brandy and mint chocolate brandy in some very inventive and delicious cocktails.

KOHLER DARK CHOCOLATE BRANDY VIEUX CARRE

Peter Kalleward, mixologist, Destination Kohler, Kohler

1¼ oz. Kohler Dark Chocolate Brandy

½ oz. Rittenhouse Rye

¼ oz. Punt e Mes vermouth

½ oz. sweet vermouth

½ oz. Tariquet VSOP Armagnac brandy

¼ oz. Benedictine liqueur

GLASS: rocks

GARNISH: lemon twist wrapped around a Luxardo cherry on a spear

Stir all ingredients together with ice until chilled, about sixty seconds. Strain into a rocks glass filled with a single ball of ice. Add garnish.

. . . .

KOHLER DARK CHOCOLATE MINT BRANDY SIDECAR

Peter Kalleward, mixologist, Destination Kohler, Kohler

1 oz. Kohler Dark Chocolate Mint Brandy

1 oz. Copper and Kings Apple Brandy

¾ oz. Pierre Ferrand Dry Curaçao

¼ oz. Barrow's Intense Ginger Liqueur

½ oz. simple syrup

¾ oz. fresh lemon juice

sugar, lemon wedge for rim

GLASS: coupe

GARNISH: large twist of lemon

Put all ingredients, except garnish and sugar, into a shaker filled with ice. Shake hard for at least sixty seconds. Prepare glass by wiping the rim with lemon wedge, then dip glass into sugar poured on a shallow dish. Double-strain into the prepared glass using a cocktail strainer and a tea strainer and garnish with a large twist of lemon placed on the rim of the glass. "We call it 'kinda like a sidecar,' the drink with sugar around the rim," says Kalleward.

. . . .

Kohler Dark Chocolate Mint Brandy Mai Tai
at Destination Kohler

Kohler Dark Chocolate Mint Brandy Sidecar
at Destination Kohler (Peter Kalleward)

KOHLER DARK CHOCOLATE MINT BRANDY MAI TAI

Peter Kalleward, mixologist, Destination Kohler, Kohler

2 oz. Kohler Dark Chocolate Mint Brandy, or other brandy
½ oz. honey simple syrup
¼ oz. Giffard Orgeat, or other orgeat

¾ oz. fresh lemon juice
¼ oz. passion fruit puree

GLASS: Collins
GARNISH: orange wheel and umbrella

Place all ingredients into a shaker filled with ice. Shake hard for at least sixty seconds. Strain into a Collins glass filled with crushed ice. Garnish with an orange wheel and umbrella.

Honey simple syrup can be made by whisking 1 cup honey into ½ cup hot water until completely dissolved.

....

A Pig with a Revolver

At A Pig in a Fur Coat in Madison, owner Bonnie Arent and her staff use everything they can for both their dishes and their drinks. They also try to change things up seasonally, and they switch cocktails on and off the menu, as seasons change and as farmers bring them different ingredients.

However, there's one drink they put on the menu that they can never take off, and that's the Revolver. Arent and bartender Akash Gupta often experiment together, and previous drinks have included peaches and bacon-infused whiskey. "We're often searching for new ideas, and one day, we found some bone marrow, and I had gotten some cognac [delivered to the restaurant] right before that," she says. "So, we experimented, and we did a batch, and it all came together. It doesn't always happen that way, but it did for this cocktail."

Lately, Arent has been experimenting with infusing cheese into cocktails. They haven't found a recipe they like well enough to add to their menu yet, but fans wouldn't be surprised if that happens soon.

And the name of the cocktail, Revolver? It's a play on Le Reviseur, the cognac they use in the cocktail.

REVOLVER

Bonnie Arent, owner, and Akash Gupta, bartender,
A Pig in a Fur Coat, Madison

2 oz. bone-marrow-infused cognac, preferably Le Reviseur

¼ oz. Ancho Reyes liqueur, or other chili liqueur

⅛ oz. honey simple syrup

2 dashes orange bitters

GLASS: snifter

Stir all ingredients together with ice until well chilled, about sixty seconds. Strain into a snifter and serve neat.

The easiest way to make bone-marrow-infused cognac is to heat 5 oz. bone marrow until just melted. Pour bone marrow into a 750 ml bottle of cognac (you may have to pour out some cognac to make room for the marrow). Let sit at room temperature for a day, then freeze, and strain out cognac.

Honey simple syrup can be made by combining equal parts honey and hot water. Stir honey into hot water until completely dissolved.

Elderflower French 75 at A Pig in a Fur Coat (A Pig in a Fur Coat)

Both the chefs and bartenders at A Pig in a Fur Coat excel at using seasonal ingredients. One reason? They have built solid relationships with local farmers around Dane County, who bring them interesting ingredients in season. One such ingredient is elderflowers. Instead of using imported elderflower liqueur for this cocktail, they make their own fresh elderflower syrup.

ELDERFLOWER FRENCH 75

Bonnie Arent, owner, A Pig in a Fur Coat, Madison

1½ oz. gin, preferably Bluecoat
½ oz. fresh lemon juice
½ oz. elderflower simple syrup
3 to 4 oz. sparkling wine

GLASS: champagne flute
GARNISH: lemon twist

Shake gin, lemon juice, and elderflower syrup with ice until chilled. Double-strain into a champagne flute using a cocktail strainer and a tea strainer, top with sparkling wine, and add lemon twist for garnish.

To make elderflower simple syrup pour 1 cup sugar, 1 cup warm water, 3 sliced lemon rounds, and a large bunch of destemmed elderflowers in a container (such as a mason jar) and stir until the sugar has completely dissolved. Let this mixture sit for two days at room temperature. If you prefer a stronger elderflower flavor, let it sit for up to four or five days.

Hard Cider and Cocktails

Walker Fanning founded Hidden Cave Cidery inside of Old Sugar Distillery in Madison. Fanning and the bartenders at Old Sugar often collaborate on cocktails, and they like taking classic cocktails and then reintroducing them to customers in a new way.

The French 75 is a classic cocktail made with gin and champagne, but instead of using champagne they use Fanning's lemongrass lavender hard cider and Old Sugar's Pomeroy apple brandy. The name? "We call it the French 608, for the area code here in Madison," Fanning says.

FRENCH 608

Walker Fanning, owner of Hidden Cave Cidery,
with bartending staff at Old Sugar Distillery, Madison

1½ oz. Old Sugar Pomeroy apple brandy, or other brandy
½ oz. simple syrup
¾ oz. fresh lemon juice
4 oz. Hidden Cave lemongrass lavender hard cider, or other hard cider

GLASS: champagne
GARNISH: lemon twist

Pour apple brandy, simple syrup, and lemon juice into a shaker filled with ice. Shake for thirty to sixty seconds, then strain into champagne glass. Top with hard cider and garnish with lemon twist if desired.

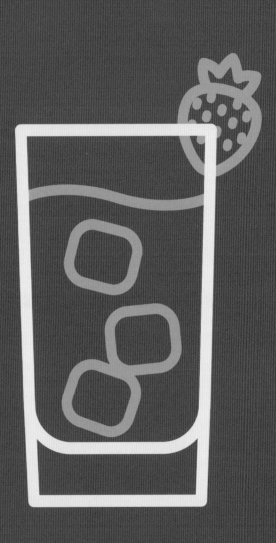

N⁰8

———

SPIRITFREE

NONALCOHOLIC COCKTAILS MADE WITH
WISCONSIN INGREDIENTS

THIS CHAPTER IS ALL ABOUT NONALCOHOLIC COCKTAILS, BUT I'D RATHER USE A DIFFERENT WORD THAN "MOCKTAIL" TO REFER TO THESE DRINKS, WHICH ARE AS DELICIOUS AND REFRESHING AS THE REST OF THE COCKTAILS IN THIS BOOK.

Instead, I'm going to use the term coined by celebrated Chicago mixologist and startender Julia Momose: spiritfree.

Momose hates the term "mocktail." Is it a mockery of a cocktail? Is it less than a cocktail? And should you be ashamed for ordering a drink that doesn't boast any booze? Momose tried out various terms— zero proof, alcohol-free, etc.—but the one she found most empowering is "spiritfree." It offers a positive connotation: that you're doing something good for you, that it is an empowering choice you're making, and that you should be proud of ordering it. And it also denotes that these mixed beverages are made with the same thought and care that goes into a regular boozy concoction. Momose is so passionate about spiritfrees that she wrote a manifesto on the subject, and she has inspired some bartenders around the globe to use the term.

So, I'm going to promote her nomenclature—because these drinks are no less than any spirited counterpart. That said, whatever you want to call them, they are delicious, and they're a great alternative if you don't or can't consume alcohol. They're great if you're not in the mood to drink, if you're the designated driver, or if you've reached your limit. You'll still feel every bit as grownup drinking them as you would a brandy Old Fashioned, a Bloody Mary, or a Manhattan.

That said, there is one big difference (outside of the alcohol) that you really need to take into account when making these concoctions.

While water—and ice—can open up a whiskey's distinctive aromas, mellow out a strong gin, or allow a brandy to breathe, it has the opposite effect on a beverage made without alcohol. Water—and ice—simply dilutes and reduces the flavors of the drink. So, what you'll want to do is chill all your elixirs before you combine them and serve with ice sparingly.

It also should be mentioned that you should make sure all your ingredients are top-notch. Good booze can cover up a lot of subpar ingredients in a drink, but when you don't have any alcohol, then second-rate ingredients will sink your drink. Use quality, as-fresh-as-possible juices. Brew your own coffee, or buy it brewed carefully from your favorite café. And if the recipe calls for it, definitely use a good tonic, seltzer, or soda.

Local Ingredients to Make Local Drinks, Starting with Fresh Fruits and Juices

While we may be known as America's Dairyland, cows (and goats and sheep, for that matter) aren't the only focus of our agriculture. Cranberries, cherries, and apples, oh my! Strawberries, raspberries, and blueberries, oh my!

We grow more cranberries than any other state, producing 60 percent of the country's crops for Thanksgiving tables everywhere, not to mention juicing it for breakfasts and cocktails everywhere. Door County cherries are famous throughout the Midwest, if not further. We also grow somewhere near 50 million pounds of apples. Not to mention some raspberries, blueberries, and even gooseberries. And a few peaches, plums, and pears, too.

Amid the more common berries, Wisconsin is also home to such delicacies as mulberries and juneberries. Juneberries, sometimes called "serviceberries," grow on small trees all over the Midwest, and they typically come in season in June or July. When they do, a local farmer brings large harvests of them to A Pig in a Fur Coat in Madison, where they get turned into shrubs for both nonalcoholic and alcoholic cocktails.

What's also really nice is the many, many farmers' markets as well as farms where you can pick your own fruits and vegetables. While using fresh fruits and juices is important to the making of any cocktail, it is doubly important when making cocktails without any booze—if there's no booze, there's nothing to cover up the cloying, sugary taste of bottled lime juice, for example.

If you don't want to juice your own, you can go online to order fresh, cold-pressed juices from Industry Juice (www.twistedalchemy .com). While this company sells primarily to bars and restaurants across the country, individuals can also buy their juice, and while the company is headquartered just across the border in northern Illinois, their actual juicing is done in Milwaukee. Besides lemon, lime, orange, and pineapple juices, they also do ruby red grapefruit, blood orange, and watermelon.

JUNEBERRY JULEP

Bonnie Arent, owner, A Pig in a Fur Coat, Madison

2 tbsp. demerara sugar
2 to 3 leaves of mint
½ oz. fresh lemon juice
1 oz. juneberry shrub
2 oz. seltzer

GLASS: rocks
GARNISH: mint

Muddle 2 to 3 leaves of mint with demerara sugar in the bottom of a shaker. Add lemon juice, juneberry shrub, and ice. Shake for thirty to sixty seconds, until just cooled. Pour into a rocks glass filled with ice, then top with seltzer and add mint for garnish.

To make this an alcoholic julep, reduce shrub to ¾ oz., add 1½ oz. Michter's Rye, and shake the rye with the other ingredients. If you add rye, eliminate the seltzer.

The juneberry shrub can be made by mixing 1 cup juneberries and 1 cup sugar in a bowl until incorporated, then pour in 1 cup champagne vinegar and stir. Let it sit, covered, at room temperature for seven days, stirring at least once, then strain. You can store for up to six months.

. . . .

HIBISCUS LEMON CUCUMBER MOCKTAIL

Josh Stender, beverage director, St. Kate's Arts Hotel, Milwaukee

3 oz. hibiscus simple syrup

3 oz. lemon juice

2 oz. cucumber water

¾ oz. rosewater

3 oz. seltzer

GLASS: coupe
GARNISH: slices of cucumber

Combine all ingredients except seltzer. Chill. Pour hibiscus mixture into two coupe glasses, top with seltzer, garnish with cucumber slices.

Hibiscus simple syrup can be made by combining ¾ cup water, ¾ cup sugar, and ¾ cup dried hibiscus flowers. Bring all ingredients to a boil. Let cool and steep for two or more hours. Strain, then chill.

To make cucumber water, combine in a glass 1 cup cold water and 1 small, seedless cucumber, roughly chopped. Refrigerate for at least two hours. Strain.

. . . .

CHERRY BLUSH

½ cup cherry juice (100 percent juice)
1 tbsp. honey
1 tsp. fresh lime juice

4 drops lime essential oil
4 oz. seltzer
4 to 5 fresh cranberries

GLASS: martini or coupe
GARNISH: lime wheel

In a large glass, stir together cherry juice, honey, lime juice, and two drops of essential oil. Add ice and seltzer, stir until chilled. Strain into martini glass, add garnish, then drizzle remaining essential oil on top.

....

RHUBARB AND STRAWBERRY GINGER ALE

Michele Price, caterer and culinary blogger, appetiteforentertaining.com, Hales Corners

1 oz. rhubarb simple syrup
1 oz. strawberry puree
3 oz. ginger ale

GLASS: Collins, rocks, or coupe
GARNISH: fresh strawberry

Chill all ingredients first. Place simple syrup and strawberry puree into a shaker filled with ice. (To make this a regular cocktail, add 1 oz. gin.) Shake for thirty seconds, strain into a chilled glass, top with ginger ale. Garnish with a strawberry.

Rhubarb simple syrup can be made by heating 1 cup water and 1 cup sugar in a saucepan over medium-high heat. Bring to a simmer, stirring frequently, until sugar dissolves. Remove from heat. Place 2½ lbs. fresh or frozen rhubarb, cut into chunks, in a large pot, pour simple syrup over rhubarb, and heat over medium-high heat. Bring to a boil and then immediately reduce heat to medium and let simmer for five minutes. Remove from heat, strain liquid, and discard solids.

Juneberry Julep at A Pig in a Fur Coat (A Pig in a Fur Coat)

Rhubarb and Strawberry Ginger Ale (Appetite for Entertaining)

To make a strawberry puree, place 1 lb. fresh, cleaned strawberries, ¼ cup sugar, ¼ cup water, and 1 tbsp. strawberry jam in blender and blend until smooth. Strain through a fine mesh strainer or cheesecloth to remove seeds.

....

MAGGIE MAY

Valerie Collins, tasting room administrator and mixologist, Cedar Ridge Winery & Distillery, Swisher, Iowa

½ oz. dark cherry juice or grenadine
2 oz. orange juice
2 oz. pineapple juice
2 to 4 oz. Sprite

GLASS: Collins
GARNISH: blood orange wheel

In a Collins glass, pour cherry juice or grenadine into the bottom, then top with crushed ice. In a separate glass, stir together orange juice and pineapple juice, and pour over ice in the first glass. Top with Sprite, and gently stir until ombre effect is achieved. Garnish with blood orange wheel.

To make this a regular cocktail, reduce pineapple and orange juices to 1 oz. each and replace with 2 oz. dark rum.

....

Maggie May (Valerie Collins)

Shrub Making

Fresh fruits are an integral ingredient in shrubs. Shrubs are basically equal parts fruit, sugar, and vinegar, and while they were quite common in the eighteenth and nineteenth centuries, especially as a way to preserve fruit, they fell by the wayside as other methods of preserving fruit, or shipping it fresh, arose. Fortunately, modern bartenders are reviving this sweet-and-sour tradition, and while it can be used in regular cocktails, it's a stellar ingredient to boost flavor if you're not using any booze. Bonnie Arent and her staff at A Pig in a Fur Coat make shrubs during the height of fruit seasons, and they work with local farmers to get the best fruit. For optimum results, Arent recommends using champagne vinegar, and if you don't have that, stick to a white wine vinegar. Other vinegars, like apple cider vinegar, can also be used, but champagne and white wine vinegars tend to work best. If you use balsamic vinegar, you will want to blend it with another vinegar because it has a very strong flavor.

Arent recommends weighing out the ingredients instead of using measuring cups. She also recommends experimentation with whatever fruit is in season.

"What you're looking for, when you make a shrub, is for the sugar and vinegar to interact with each other to mellow each other out," Arent says. "After it mellows, it will taste like vinegar, but it won't have that mouth-puckering sour taste. It's a pleasant mouthfeel."

Arent says to let the shrub mellow for about a week; some bartenders only let it meld for about half a day. I recommend tasting the shrub as it goes along so that you discover how sour or sweet you like it, and make the shrub to your own personal preferences.

Seasonal shrubs and syrups (see chapter 7 for elderflower simple syrup) can be combined together, with some fresh lemon or lime juice, and a bubbly beverage like seltzer or ginger beer and you've got a nonalcoholic beverage that's sparkling with flavor. "Using shrubs and syrups is a lot of fun," Arent says.

BLUEBERRY SOUR

½ oz. blueberry shrub
½ oz. simple syrup
½ oz. freshly squeezed lemon juice
3 to 4 oz. club soda or seltzer

GLASS: Collins, rocks, or martini
GARNISH: lemon peel and three fresh blueberries

In a large glass filled with ice, stir together blueberry shrub, simple syrup, and lemon juice. Strain into glass, top with seltzer or club soda, garnish with lemon peel and fresh blueberries.

The blueberry shrub can be made by stirring together ½ cup fresh or frozen wild blueberries, ½ cup sugar, and ½ cup white balsamic vinegar in a small bowl. Cover with plastic wrap. Let it sit at room temperature or in the refrigerator for at least twelve hours or up to seven days. Strain out blueberries and use.

....

Coffee

Wisconsin's coffee culture and coffee roasters are as good as if not better than anywhere else in the world. While we don't grow coffee locally, we roast it all around the state. And most of our baristas know that coffee can be a secret ingredient in nonalcoholic beverages. And not just in lattes and the sweet or cold coffee concoctions you can find in chain cafés: coffee can add subtle flavors, mouthfeel, and aromas to replace those created by booze in beverages.

Wolfgang Schaefer, owner of Uncle Wolfie's Breakfast Tavern in Milwaukee, started out his career in beverages as a barista. He became so good at it that he became the educator and beverage guru of Anodyne Coffee. He left Anodyne to start an old-fashioned breakfast tavern, where he shakes up not only inventive regular cocktails but beverages with a different kind of buzz.

BLOODY MARY COFFEE COCKTAIL

Wolfgang Schaefer, owner, Uncle Wulfie's Breakfast Tavern, Milwaukee

2½ oz. homemade Bloody Mary mix
2 oz. Anodyne's Dark Columbia Tolima cold-brew coffee concentrate
1½ oz. Fever Tree ginger beer
20 drops Bittercube Jamaican No. 1 bitters

GLASS: tall Collins or pint
GARNISH: Pernat's honey barbecue stick, Wisconsin cheese curds, lemon wedge, lime wedge, and anise sprig

Combine all ingredients in a shaker filled with ice. Lightly shake. Pour into a tall Collins or pint glass rimmed with honey and jerk seasoning. Garnish with Pernat's honey barbecue stick, Wisconsin cheese curds, lemon wedge, lime wedge, and a sprig or two of anise.

While you can buy cold-brew coffee concentrates from coffee roasters and at grocery stores, you can easily make it yourself. Simply combine 2 tbsp. coarse-ground coffee beans with one cup of water. Let stand overnight or up to twenty-four hours. Strain out grounds and use.

COFFEE JULEP

Wolfgang Schaefer, owner, Uncle Wulfie's Breakfast Tavern, Milwaukee

1 to 2 tsp. honey

7 to 10 fresh mint leaves

¼ oz. fresh lime juice

2 shots of espresso

3 oz. Fever Tree tonic, or other tonic

GLASS: short Collins or rocks

GARNISH: sprig of mint

Lightly muddle mint and honey. Make espresso. Cool shots of espresso in small water bath for about one minute (too hot espresso will make the mint bitter). Add cooled espresso and lime juice to shaker with ice. Shake very lightly. Pour slowly into short Collins or rocks glass already filled with tonic. Garnish with mint.

. . . .

HORCHATA COLD BREW

Rachel Werner, digital media artist, fitness model, and writer, Madison

32 oz. organic almond milk

½ can of coconut milk, full-fat (use whole can if using light milk)

5 tbsp. ground cinnamon or 3 cinnamon sticks

3 tbsp. vanilla extract

¼ cup maple syrup or agave

2 tbsp. honey

1 cup Wisconsin cold-brew coffee, preferably Cadence or Let It Ride

GLASS: Collins

GARNISH: none needed but a sprinkle of cinnamon or a cinnamon stick if desired

Whisk the maple syrup, honey, and vanilla extract together in small bowl. Then combine all remaining ingredients in a large pitcher or container (just be sure whichever container chosen has a lid). Add the sweetener mixture and stir vigorously for three to four minutes. Whisk well to blend. Best if chilled overnight before consuming, but in a pinch can be served the same day by blending well with one to two cups of ice. Makes four servings.

. . . .

Tonics

Mary Pellettieri, who holds a masters in occupational and environmental health and has a bachelors degree in botany, started her spirited career by working on the brewing side of things. She oversaw quality control and beverage development for Goose Island Beer Co. in Chicago and then was lured away to Milwaukee by Miller-Coors to work in a senior corporate position.

Pellettieri originally thought she'd start her own craft brewing company and make herbal beers, but as she got into herbs and tonics her interest shifted. In 2014 she started La Pavia Beverage Co. to make her line of Top Note beverage concentrates. "I thought the soft drink and tonic business just seems more interesting, and this alcohol-adjacent space seemed to be the next place where innovation's going to take place," Pellettieri says. "I'd been in beer for more than twenty years, and I didn't want to be in a saturated place."

"When we were at the Fancy Food Show, people would come up to our booth and say 'This is the only tonic I can drink.' You're turning people on to the category," she recalls. "Far too many tonics just use quinine. I view bitters differently. There are too many products that taste the same but just have a different label. That's boring to me."

Her Indian Tonic is an exciting example. Instead of a tonic that uses only quinine as a bittering agent, she combines it with gentian root so the resulting cocktails made with her tonic are more complex. "We want to show that there are different ways of bittering," she says.

Her current lineup has evolved, and instead of selling just tonic concentrates, she sells bottled bittered beverages. Besides Indian

Tonic, she also makes Bitter Lemon Tonic and Ginger Beer—and she sells soda mixers, including a grapefruit, a classic lemon-lime tonic, and a lemon cuke sour, which combines savory cucumber and celery with sour. Though she started with mixers, now all her beverages come carbonated and they're available in both glass bottles and cans.

"Mixers are fun," she says. "People shouldn't be afraid to make cocktails at home, especially with a better mixer. I always challenge people—if you're going to buy a tonic, buy a good tonic, and have a much better experience."

And though this is a chapter on spiritfrees, it must be mentioned that all her tonics make delicious gin and tonics, too.

NO BOOZE OLD FASHIONED

Mary Pellettieri

1 oz. Top Note Bitter Orange syrup
1½ oz. orange juice
3 oz. seltzer
1 bar spoon cherry juice (optional)

GLASS: rocks
GARNISH: cherry and orange

Stir all ingredients together with ice until chilled.

If Top Note Bitter Orange syrup is not available, suitable substitutes are 4 oz. of Top Note grapefruit soda or 4 oz. of Top Note Bitter Lemon tonic. It will have a slightly different flavor, but it will still taste delicious.

. . . .

No Booze Old Fashioned (Jim Moy for Top Note Tonics)

Nonalcoholic Cosmo at The Cheel

G-LESS T COCKTAIL

4 oz. tonic, preferably Top Note   ¾ oz. cucumber water
1¼ oz. Death-less Door simple syrup

GLASS: tall Collins
GARNISH: cucumber slice spread with Blue Jay blue cheese

Chill all ingredients for at least two hours. Pour all ingredients into a glass with ice. Briskly stir for thirty to sixty seconds. Strain into a glass and add garnish.

Death-less Door simple syrup can be made by combining 1½ cups organic sugar and 1 cup water. Bring to a boil. Add ¼ cup chopped fresh fennel, 2 tbsp. juniper berries, and 2 tbsp. whole coriander and boil for two minutes. Turn off heat and let steep for two hours. After cooled and steeped, use the back of a spoon or measuring cup to gently press juniper berries. Strain.

To make cucumber water, combine in a glass 1 cup cold water and 1 small, seedless cucumber, roughly chopped. Refrigerate for at least two hours. Strain.

....

Speaking of Booze

Though this is a chapter on nonalcoholic beverages, most recipes here can be tweaked to become regular cocktails if you so desire. If you prefer to imbibe a regular cocktail, my recommendation is to start by adding just ¾ oz. to 1½ oz. of the spirit of your choice to the nonalcoholic drink. Add the alcohol, shake or stir, then taste. Since these nonalcoholic creations are already carefully balanced, adding too much booze will unbalance them and cause them to taste less than delicious—so you may have to add additional ice or citrus or simple syrup to rebalance them.

NONALCOHOLIC COSMO

Drew Kassner, general manager and head mixologist,
The Cheel, Thiensville

1½ oz. cranberry juice
1½ oz. Amilo sour mix
1 oz. water
½ oz. orange juice

GLASS: martini or coupe
GARNISH: lemon twist

Shake all ingredients together with ice for about twenty seconds until chilled. Strain into a chilled martini glass, garnish with a lemon twist.

Amilo sour mix can be made by whisking together 1 cup fresh lemon juice, 1 cup fresh lime juice, 1 cup sugar, and 1 cup hot water until sugar is dissolved.

....

NONALCOHOLIC KATMANDU 75

Drew Kassner, general manager and head mixologist,
The Cheel, Thiensville

1 oz. water
1 oz. fresh lemon juice
¾ oz. rosemary simple syrup
1 dropper of Bittercube Jamaica No. 1 bitters, or other bitters
1½ oz. Fevertree ginger beer

GLASS: coupe
GARNISH: rosemary sprig and dried lemon wheel

Place all ingredients, except ginger beer, into a shaker filled with ice. Shake for ten seconds, strain into coupe glass, top with ginger beer and garnishes.

Rosemary simple syrup can be made by putting 2 cups hot water, 2 cups sugar, 4 rosemary sprigs (stems removed), and ¼ tsp. salt into a blender. Blend until smooth, then strain.

....

NONALCOHOLIC YETI

Drew Kassner, general manager and head mixologist, The Cheel, Thiensville

2 oz. water
1 oz. spiced simple syrup
¾ oz. fresh lemon juice
1 full dropper Bittercube Jamaican No. 2 bitters, or other bitters
2 oz. ginger beer or seltzer

GLASS: coupe
GARNISH: dehydrated lemon wheel

Place all ingredients, except ginger beer or seltzer, in a shaker filled with ice. Shake for about ten seconds, strain into a chilled coupe glass, top with ginger beer or seltzer, garnish with dehydrated lemon wheel.

The easiest way to make spiced simple syrup is to toast spices—1 stick cinnamon, 1 tsp. black cardamom, 1 tsp. green cardamom, ½ tsp. ground cloves, ½ tsp. black peppercorns—over medium-high heat until fragrant, then grind. Whisk ground spices, 1 cup hot water, 1 cup honey, and 1 cup sugar together until sugar is dissolved, then strain.

APPENDIX

WISCONSIN COCKTAIL AND CHEESE PAIRINGS

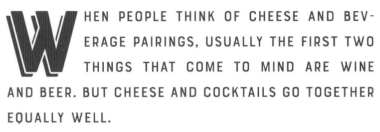

WHEN PEOPLE THINK OF CHEESE AND BEV-
ERAGE PAIRINGS, USUALLY THE FIRST TWO
THINGS THAT COME TO MIND ARE WINE
AND BEER. BUT CHEESE AND COCKTAILS GO TOGETHER
EQUALLY WELL.

And if there are two things we do exceptionally well in Wisconsin, it's making cheese and making cocktails—so I think the pairing is a natural. I've taught several cocktail and cheese pairings classes, where I've coupled some stellar Wisconsin cheeses with Wisconsin cocktails—and not just a Bloody Mary topped with some cheese curds.

"Cheese and spirits is actually one of my favorite pairings," says Liz Henry, who co-owns J. Henry & Sons Bourbon with her husband, Joe, in Dane.

Henry should know about cheese and cocktail pairings because not only does she make bourbon grown with her family-grown corn but she also—almost forty years ago—was Alice in Dairyland. She started pairing her family's bourbon and bourbon cocktails when she did a popup a few years ago with Sassy Cow eggnog.

Cheese and cocktail pairings, she says, should be something to savor. "It's all about bringing out the flavors in both," she says.

Getting Cheesy

Before delving a bit deeper into the realm of cheese and cocktail pairings, here's a brief primer on Wisconsin cheese: while America's Dairyland lost its milk mantle to California years ago, Wisconsin still makes more cheese than any other state. In fact, if Wisconsin were its own country, it would be the fourth largest cheese-producing region in the world, behind the rest of the United States, Germany, and France. In 2017, we produced more than 3.42 billion pounds of cheese (California, the second-ranked state, produced 2.5 billion pounds). We have nearly two thousand licensed cheesemakers, and we have the most rigorous licensing program for cheesemakers in the country. We have the only master cheesemakers certification program in the country—to become a master, a cheesemaker has to have been making a cheese for at least five years, and then has to go through a rigorous period of study, testing, and judging that goes on for another three years.

Wisconsin makes more than one thousand different types of dairy products—and most of them are cheeses. We produce more specialty cheese than anywhere else in the country. We produce more Cheddar than any other state, and we also produce more blue cheeses than anywhere else (more Gouda and Limburger, too).

And while our cows might not produce as much liquid milk as California's bovines, our goats and sheep produce more milk than any other state.

What this means is that in Wisconsin, when it comes to cheese, we're spoiled—good cheese can be found in pretty much every grocery store, plenty of gas stations, and when you're driving through practically every corner of the state you'll find cheese stores at actual creameries and farms.

But for pairing purposes, what you need is a bit of information about the types of cheeses and their properties. Cheeses fall into these different categories:

Fresh cheeses are unaged cheeses like Mozzarella, Chevre, and Quark. They're creamy, young, and almost juicy, and they contain more whey than other cheeses. Burrata and Mascarpone are also fresh cheeses.

Bloomy rind and triple crème cheeses are those lovely, creamy cheeses with the white rinds on the outside. Think Brie, Camembert, and in Wisconsin you also have some American originals (cheeses without any European counterparts) like Martone. They're luscious, they often are made with extra cream, and they usually taste delicious when they're baked with jams, fruits, or nuts.

Washed-rind cheeses (aka stinky cheeses) are those aromatic beauties like Taleggio and Limburger. They're named for the process cheesemakers use to create them—they actually wash the rinds. While their smell might be an acquired liking, they usually taste pretty mild and are sometimes similar in texture, if not taste, to bloomy rinds. In Wisconsin, an American original in this category is Monroe.

Semisoft cheeses are young, lightly aged cheeses. Think Colby, young Goudas, and young Havartis. I would also add young and mild Cheddars to this category.

Firm cheeses, which often can be thrown in with hard cheeses, are the Swiss-style cheeses: Gruyere, Emmentaler, and Beaufort, as well as the Spanish Manchego. In Wisconsin, you'll also have Pleasant Ridge Reserve, Gran Canaria, and Bellavitano. Most aged Cheddars fall into this category, too, but I think the twenty-year-old Cheddars probably should be considered in the next category. In general, firm cheeses often have nutty or fruity aromas, and they are great when melted into fondues or cheese sandwiches.

Hard cheeses are the big boys and girls of the cheese world. Dry, hard, grainy, crunchy, and crumbly, these cheeses often win big in national and international cheese competitions. Think Italian aged Parmigiano-Reggiano, dry Monterey Jacks, aged Cheddars, and aged Goudas. They usually have complex flavors, and a little bit goes a long way. In Wisconsin, we have a lot of fantastic Italian-style aged cheeses, as well as fifteen- and even twenty-year-old Cheddars.

Blue cheeses can be creamy and spreadable or crumbly and slightly hard, but what they all have in common are strains of penicillium molds used to ripen them. Besides the Gorgonzolas and Roqueforts of the world, in Wisconsin we also have Buttermilk Blue, Ewe Calf to Be Kidding Me, Blue Jay, Billy Blue, Ba Ba Blue, and many others. Blue cheeses are strong and full of flavor, and when you add a dollop of honey or jam, it brings out their inherent sweetness.

Mixed-milk cheeses aren't exactly a separate category, but in Wisconsin a lot of our cheesemakers combine more than one type of milk to make cheese. Carr Valley's Gran Canaria, for example, combines sheep, goat, and cow milks, as does Hook's Ewe Calf to Be Kidding Me, while Martone combines goat and cow milks. They can fall into any category of cheese, but what's interesting is how the different milks impart different characteristics to the cheeses.

Processed cheeses aren't exactly cheese—they're cheese products. American cheese and Velveeta fall into this category, but so do cheese spreads. While I'm not a fan of processed cheese in general, a

Big Ed's Gouda cheese spread, a well-crafted Provolone and chianti spread, and a fine Cheddar spread just taste great. If you want to make your own cheese spread, check out the Fromage Fort recipe at the end of the appendix.

Two Basic Pairing Approaches

Evan Topel, executive chef for Emmi Roth Cheese in Monroe, says there are two trains of thought when it comes to pairing. "The first train is to do something that complements the flavors of each, and the other train of thought is to do the opposite, like sweet and salty are opposites," he says.

If he's thinking about a Bloody Mary, for example, Topel likes his spicy, so he looks for a spicy cheese like a horseradish and chive Havarti. For a contrasting experience, one of his favorites is to take a Golden Cadillac, a classic ice cream drink (see recipe in chapter 4), with a cave-aged blue cheese. A complementing cheese to that same ice cream drink would be a Mascarpone or a Burrata with honey. "I could also see a Burrata with a Manhattan as a real opposite pairing," he says.

Sheana Davis, a chef in California who adores Wisconsin cheeses and often uses them in her catering company, The Epicurean Connection, says that nutty cheeses—the Roth's Private Reserve, the Pleasant Ridge Reserves, the Edelweiss Creamery Emmentaler cheeses—all go really well with fruity flavored cocktails. One of her favorite examples is to take Emmi Roth's Gran Cru or Emmi Roth's Private Reserve and top it with pecans and a drizzle of pomegranate molasses. "You can get pomegranate molasses everywhere now at places like Target and Trader Joe's," she says.

Davis then serves that with a Bourbon and Pomegranate Cocktail (recipe at end of appendix). "This also translates quite nicely to a mocktail—you just leave out the bourbon," she says.

Henry says that drier, aged cheeses—the ones with lactate crystals—pair beautifully with straight bourbon and bourbon-based cocktails. "There's something magical about those crystals," she says. "Take a little bite of the cheese, then move it around in your mouth. Then take a little sip of bourbon, and then leave bourbon in your mouth, and then take a little bite of cheese, and those crystals explode like pop rocks in your mouth. It's just delicious."

Henry says it's an example of a perfect pairing. "The flavors of both the cheese and the bourbon are broader and bigger and more enhanced," she says.

Creamier cheeses like Brie or La Clare Farm's Martone, fresh Chevre or Hidden Springs Creamery's Driftless creamy sheep's milk cheeses all go really well with champagne and sparkling wine-based cocktails like the French 608 (chapter 7), the Spring Champagne Cocktail (chapter 6), and the Champagne Cocktail (recipe at end of appendix). Hidden Springs Lavender and Honey Driftless would go really well with the Lavender and Honey Gin Gimlet (recipe at end of appendix). "Hook's Ewe Calf to Be Kidding Me blue cheese would also go well with any gin or vodka drinks," she says. "Blue cheese goes with anything made with gin or vodka."

Booze-Laced Cheese Makes Pairings Easy

Some perfect cheese and booze pairings are made easier—because some Wisconsin cheesemakers add booze or elements related to booze to their cheeses. Deer Creek, for example, makes an eighteen-month-old Cheddar cheese called Night Walker that has been rubbed with a five-year-old J. Henry bourbon. This cheese obviously goes well with any bourbon or whiskey-based cocktails, including Old Fashioneds and Manhattans. Other Wisconsin cheeses made with booze or ingredients conducive to booze include:

Sartori's cognac-washed Bellavitano—all brandy and cognac-based cocktails such as Old Fashioneds, Sidecars, etc.

Deer Creek's Moon Rabbit, which is rubbed with chartreuse—any chartreuse-based cocktails, including Wisconsin's Last Word.

Deer Creek's Rattlesnake, a Cheddar laced with tequila and hot peppers—Bloody Mary and Bloody Maria cocktails, as well as any other spicy cocktails.

Sartori's raspberry ale-washed Bellavitano—any raspberry cocktails, including Raspberry Russian.

Deer Creek's Blue Jay blue cheese with juniper berries—any and all gin-based cocktails like Martinis and Gimlets. It goes amazingly well with a Gin Cosmo.

Carr Valley's Vanilla Cardona—any whiskey-based cocktails in which the whiskey has notes of vanilla.

Carr Valley's Cocoa Cardona—any chocolate or coffee-based cocktails, such as Orange White Russian.

Merlot-rubbed Bellavitano—any sangrias or other fruity cocktails.

Chai-rubbed Bellavitano—any chai liqueur cocktails and chai tea-based cocktails.

Hennings Hatch-pepper-laced Cheddar—goes amazingly well with Bloody Marys, as do any of the spicy Cheddars, Havartis, bricks and other flavored Wisconsin cheeses. Black pepper-rubbed Bellavitano is another cheese that works well in Bloody Marys.

Bridging Everything Together

Another element to consider when pairing cheese and cocktails is to add a bridge. A bridge is an element that brings a beverage and a food together—chefs and sommeliers do this all the time at wine dinners. A wine with cherry aromas will be paired up with a pork tenderloin that is served with a cherry sauce—the cherry acts as a bridge between the wine and the pork. For cheese and cocktail pairings or cheese and spirits, take the basic aromas of the spirit that the cocktail is based on. For gin, for example, look at the botanicals that the gin might have—if there's lemon or orange notes, then add a lemon curd or an orange marmalade to top the cheese, and that curd or marmalade acts as a bridge.

The bridge can also be built on the flavors of the cocktail; a brandy Old Fashioned can have a bridge made of cherry jam or orange marmalade or both to tie the cheese to the cocktail. And a blackberry sour, for example, can have blackberry jam added as a bridge. "Add some raspberry jam to the cheese as a condiment, and serve it with a raspberry cocktail," Topel says. "You could even add a bit of the jam to the cocktail, too, to tie it all together."

You could, for example, serve a Raspberry Russian with a raspberry ale–washed Bellavitano cheese, with a dollop of raspberry jam.

Topel says he loves to add toasted pecans to blue cheese and serve it with a bourbon-based cocktail, as many bourbons pair so well with pecans.

Davis says that cheeses with fruity flavors—a lot of mixed-milk cheeses that Sid Cook makes at Carr Valley—go really well with tropical drinks. His Gran Canaria would go well with the Green Goose. "We've served Bessie's Blend with dried mango, and any Wisconsin *juustoleipa* [bread cheese] grilled and served with rum sauce goes with rum drinks," she says. "The Gran Canaria would go well with a mai tai."

Henry loves serving a good Manhattan with baked Brie served with a spicy chutney and maybe some plain water crackers. "The spicy chutney goes with the vermouth of the Manhattan," she says, and the strength of the cocktail is cut by the creaminess of the cheese.

Cheddars in Wisconsin come in all different ages, from mild and unaged to Hook's twenty-year-old. Milder, sweeter Cheddars pair easily with brandy cocktails and other sweeter cocktails. But the big, aged Cheddars and the Cheddars that have strains of blue, like Roelli Cheese Red Rock, need cocktails with some heft.

If you're going to pair a twenty-year-old (which costs more than $200 per pound) or even a fifteen-year-old Cheddar, you're probably going to want to have a cocktail made with an expensive, aged spirit—either whiskey or brandy or something with the word "reserve" in the name.

Spicy Cheddars and spicy Jacks go well with tequila-based cocktails and Bloody Marys. And any cheese with horseradish goes well with a Bloody Mary that's made with horseradish in its mix.

When starting out on your cocktails-and-cheese journey, Henry recommends picking three different cheeses that you like, and trying each cheese with the same cocktail. Then take notes about what you like and didn't like about the pairings. "The fact that you took a moment to notice means you're on your journey," she says. "Hopefully, you'll take it one step further to decide what you like about it. But pairings are not about being a snob or being exclusive—they're about enjoying a pleasant experience."

Serving Suggestions

While you can just add a hunk of cheese directly to your cocktail or put a piece of cheese on a plate next to the glass, presentation counts, and there are many elegant ways to garnish cheese alongside your cocktail.

For example, when you serve cheese with your Bloody Mary, Davis recommends cutting it into a triangle wedge, then cutting the wedge two-thirds of the way so you can hang it right on the glass. Davis also recommends using a breadstick of *justoleipa* bread cheese, served warm, with a Bloody Mary.

Cheese wedges and slices can also be wrapped in charcuterie. Firm and hard cheeses can be delicately sliced using a vegetable peeler, and then that delicate, long peel of cheese can be laid across the top of a cocktail glass. A slice of cheese can also be laid on top of a slice of fresh baguette, with or without a dab of honey or jam, and then the whole laid on top of the cocktail glass, as tapas are served in bars throughout Spain.

Blue cheeses, fresh Chevre, and other fresh cheeses can be stuffed into olives, tomatoes, and small peppers, and into berries, cherries, and dried apricots. These same cheeses can also be molded into little balls and skewered between dried cherries or dried cranberries. You can also put a dollop of these cheeses, with a drizzle of honey or syrup or jam, into ceramic soup spoons, and serve them alongside your cocktails.

Dip the rim of your cocktail glass into honey and then roll it into grated cheese for a sweet and cheesy rim. For a Bloody Mary, you could also roll the rim into a spice blend.

Or you could simply create a cheese plate of your favorite cheeses and accouterments and then serve it with cocktails. The choices and pairings are meant to be fun. And don't worry if your personal pairing preferences don't match the perceived perfection of professionals— your palate is your palate. Don't explain, just enjoy, and go with what you like.

BOURBON AND POMEGRANATE COCKTAIL

served with Emmi Roth's Gran Cru, Edelweiss Creamery's Emmentaler, or Uplands' Pleasant Ridge Reserve, by Sheana Davis of the Epicurean Connection

½ oz. pomegranate molasses

1 oz. pomegranate juice

2 oz. bourbon

1 dash Angostura bitters, or other bitters

1 oz. ginger ale

GLASS: rocks

GARNISH: cherry

Stir all ingredients together in a cocktail glass with ice. Strain over ice, and garnish with a cherry. Serve with aged cheese.

. . . .

CHAI BOURBON SOUR

served with Chai Bellavitano, by Sheana Davis of the Epicurean Connection

2 oz. bourbon

1 oz. lemon juice

1 oz. chai simple syrup

1 dash orange bitters

splash of sparkling lemon water, about ½ to 1 oz.

GLASS: martini or coupe

GARNISH: Chai Bellavitano

Shake all ingredients, except sparkling water, for about thirty seconds. Strain into martini or coupe glass, top with sparkling water. Garnish with wedge of Chai Bellavitano. For a more pronounced chai flavor, add ¼ to ½ oz. Twisted Path chai liqueur.

To make chai simple syrup, combine one cup chai tea with one cup sugar. Stir until sugar dissolved.

. . . .

CHAMPAGNE COCKTAIL

served with bloomy rind cheeses, fresh Chevre, or blended
fresh cheeses, by Sheana Davis of the Epicurean Connection

1½ to 2 oz. liqueur of your choice (raspberry, orange, cranberry, etc.)
4 oz. champagne or sparkling wine

GLASS: champagne
GARNISH: cheese

Pour liqueur in the bottom of champagne glass. Top with champagne or
sparkling wine. Serve with cheese.

A particularly perfect pairing would be Good Land's Cranberry liqueur
served with Driftless cranberry and cinnamon cheese or a cranberry
Cheddar or Chevre.

....

LAVENDER AND HONEY GIN GIMLET

served with Lavender and Honey Driftless

1½ oz. aromatic gin
¾ oz. fresh lemon or lime juice
¾ oz. lavender and honey simple syrup

GLASS: coupe
GARNISH: cheese

Place all ingredients in a shaker filled with ice and shake for thirty to
sixty seconds. Strain into coupe glass. Serve with cheese.

Lavender and honey simple syrup can be made by combining 1 cup
honey, 1 cup water, and 1 tbsp. dried lavender blossoms in a saucepan.
Simmer over medium-high heat for five minutes, then remove from
heat. Once cooled, strain out lavender blossoms.

....

FROMAGE FORT

to be paired with a cocktail using the wine or spirit in the recipe

½ lb. leftover cheese bits, preferably more than one type, grated or cut into small
    pieces
1 cup unsalted butter, softened
¼ to ½ cup white wine or spirit (rum, bourbon, and brandy work well)
1 to 2 cloves garlic, minced
sea salt and freshly ground pepper to taste

Place cheese, butter, ¼ cup wine or spirit, and garlic in a high-speed
blender or a food processor fitted with a standard blade. Blend until
smooth and creamy. Season with salt and pepper to taste, and then add
more wine or spirit if you so desire. Blend or process again until smooth
and creamy.

. . . .